Endorsements

Money Matters: in My Kingdom

"After hearing Bob Weimer's endorsement of Martin Powell's book *Money Matters: in My Kingdom,* I was expecting it to be awesome, but I was still surprised by how good it actually was. *This is the best book I've ever read on secular or Christian finance."*
Rick Joyner, MorningStar Ministries

"Many books have been written on prosperity, but few authors have linked the idea of prosperity to a God given plan that will advance God's Kingdom. Like a skillful surgeon, Pastor Martin cuts through all the inaccurate mindsets concerning prosperity and equips the reader to become a fine-tuned custodian of God's power to create wealth. Pastor Martin has written a masterpiece to prepare the character of God's people for the greatest transfer of wealth which will influence society with the Gospel of the Kingdom. The principles and patterns in this book will encourage you to take the necessary steps to reconfigure your mindsets in alignment with God's purpose for your life. *Money Matters: in My Kingdom* is an anointed map that will guide you into the ways of provision to fulfill God's vision for your life. Enjoy!"
Mark Kauffman, Jubilee Ministries International, Global Mega Impact Corporation, New Castle, Pennsylvania

"Martin Powell explains very clearly what the world is facing today regarding global economics and the risks we all face. Martin provides a simple concept of how to prepare for the future and to be the stewards that God has called each of us to be with our resources."
Lt. General (R) William G. Boykin, U.S. Army

"What a joy to recommend Martin Powell's new book *Money Matters: in My Kingdom.* I believe it is one of the best I have ever read on the subject of Biblical Finance! I have studied hours on many occasions in this book and have been so edified. Martin clearly understands God's original great commission listed in Genesis 12:3, that though Abraham and his seed every nation would be blessed. We are Abraham's seed given the power to make wealth so that every nation would be blessed and every person could hear the good news of Jesus. Thank you, Martin, for your wonderful book filled with practical revelation which clearly lays out a plan of action for these exciting days ahead. Everything we need has already been given in the spiritual world by our wonderful Heavenly Father before the foundation of the world by His wonderful grace, and all we have to do is walk by faith and not by sight, and everything He has already provided will be released now into our lives! Blessings!"
Bob Weiner, Weiner International

"This book is a ground breaking revelation based on the sound principle of God's word and practical experience gained through many years of working with God. I recommend to every believer desiring to stand on sound principles and to enjoy the benefits of God's prosperity to get a copy of this book. Pastor Martin Powell has given us a greater insight while also helping us to come back to basics and prosperity God's way."
Bishop Simon Iheanacho, Presiding Bishop, UK World Evangelism Churches

"Biblical prosperity is the covenant birthright of every disciple of Christ. Martin Powell has threaded the needle to deliver balanced teaching keys and understanding to point us to not only prosperity, but stewardship.
Dr. Bruce Cook, Convener, KEYS, Austin, Texas

Bravo! Pastor Powell has written an eloquent, well-balanced, and Scripturally-based treatise on a topic which oftentimes lends itself to extremism within the church. But, to characterize this book as one that teaches solely on prosperity, would be doing it a great disservice as it covers many fundamental tenets of Christianity itself. I highly recommend it to all believers."
Peter Han, Co-Founder Investingwithinsight.com, entrepreneur, consultant, and investor

"Martin Powell addresses key issues with a genuine concern for biblical truth. In a world where financial opinions abound, it is good to have a strong foundation in God's word."
Dr. Hugh Osgood, President, Churches in Communities International

Money Matters:
in My Kingdom

Study Guide

By

Martin Powell

Money Matters: in My Kingdom - Study Guide

Kingdom Talents Publishing
375 Star Light Drive
Fort Mill, SC 29715   USA

ISBN 978-1482718508

Printed in the United States of America

We would love to hear from you, and welcome your comments and thoughts about this book. If you desire Martin to come and minister the Word of God and perform his music in your Church, please mention this when you write.

To correspond with Pastor Martin Powell, please send your letter via email to: Martin@Kingdom-Talents.com.

Dedicated To

Jesus

and

Janet Powell

Special Thanks To:

Louise Allen
Gwen Cattron
Rick & DeniseAnn Crenshaw
Norma Aguilar
Alan & NancyKate Gordon
Rob Robinson
Marc Sinclair

Table of Contents

Preface

We are in unprecedented financial turmoil as the earth goes through the birth pains of the revealing of the sons of God and the ushering in of the new age, the Millennium, when Jesus will reign from Jerusalem.

Let us not fall by ignorance of His Word, but be mighty in deeds for Him who is indeed worthy.

Some of us will die for our testimonies, myself included, and others will rise up determined to preach the truth of the gospel of Christ.

Stand in the truth, and after you have done all to stand, stand.

Introduction

Money Matters: in My Kingdom- Study Guide has been compiled from years of preaching notes and Bible studies that I have written. As a result, occasionally the reader will find some repetition of material. I felt it would conflict with the integrity of the individual chapters if I were to remove the repetitious material from the text. Therefore, I have retained it in the hope that the repetition will serve to emphasize the key points in the teaching.

This study guide is not a get-rich-quick book. Rather, it aims to set out the principles through which God prospers His people. Please remember, if you want to get rich quick, you may find that you will ultimately shipwreck your faith!

We find many warnings about trying to get rich quickly throughout the Bible. Let's take a look at some of them:

> *"A faithful man will abound with blessings, but whoever **hastens to be rich** will not go unpunished."*
> *(Proverbs 28:20 NKJV)*

> *"So are the ways of every one that is **greedy of gain**; which taketh away the life of the owners thereof."*
> *(Proverbs 1:19 KJV)*

> *"Let your character be free from **the love** of money, being content with what you have; for He Himself has said, 'I will never desert you, nor will I ever forsake you.'"*
> *(Hebrews 13:5 NASB)*

> *5b " . . men of corrupt minds and destitute of the truth, **who suppose that godliness is a means of gain**. From such withdraw yourself.*
> *6 But godliness with contentment is great gain.*
> *7 For we brought nothing into this world, and it is certain we can carry nothing out.*
> *8 And having food and clothing, with these we shall be content.*
> *9 But **those who desire to be rich** fall into temptation and a snare, and into many foolish and harmful lusts which drown men in destruction and perdition.*
> *10 For **the love of money is a root of all kinds of evil**."*
> *(1Timothy 6:5-10 NKJV)*

> *24 "No one can serve two masters; for either he will hate the one and love the other, or else he will be loyal to the one and despise the other. **You cannot serve God and mammon**.*
> *25 Therefore I say to you, do not worry about your life, what you will eat or what you will drink...*

32 For after all these things the Gentiles seek. For your heavenly Father knows that you need all these things.
33 ***But seek first the kingdom of God and His righteousness****, and all these things shall be added to you."*
(Matthew 6:24-33 KJV)

We have many warnings from the Bible about the love of money and trying to get rich quickly. Certainly there is nothing wrong with being rich, but our hearts need to be pure. We must follow God's priorities, and He commands us to *"Seek first the Kingdom of God."* We cannot serve both mammon and God. *(See Matthew 6:24.)* We must make the right choices. When we choose to put God's kingdom first, we will be able to prosper.

In order to further the Kingdom of God, His children must prosper. In this way money will be made available for multitudes of ministries, whether it is a television or radio ministry, an overseas evangelism crusade, a hospital, a Christian school, a Bible college, or any other type of outreach. Money will be available to advance the Kingdom of God when His children prosper financially by seeking first His Kingdom in their lives.

The majority of us spend many hours a week in an effort to earn money, so let us be wise by taking heed to the true wisdom of how to prosper, through believing the Scriptures that God has set forth in His Word.

What is God's Heart on Prosperity?
Chapter One – Study Guide

Opening Prayer

      Dear Father, I really do want to understand biblical finances, and I ask that you would teach me from your Word. I lay my own thoughts and opinions down, and ask that you would reveal your heart on prosperity to me. I ask this in the name of Jesus. Amen.

The following questions will be answered during study of this chapter:
1. What is God's heart for true prosperity?
2. What do we use to enter the promises of God's kingdom?
3. What provisions were made for prosperity in the life of Jesus?
4. What happened when Jesus sacrificed his life for us?

God's Heart

1. What is God's heart with regard to prosperity? Does He want us to prosper, or does He want us to live a life of poverty? *(Fill in the three missing words in the scripture below.)*

      "Let them shout for joy, and be glad, that favour my righteous cause: yea, let them say continually, Let the LORD be magnified, _____ _____ _____ in the prosperity of his servant."
(Psalms 35:27 KJV)

2. What is it that the LORD gains from 'the prosperity of his servant'?

_____

3. With that in mind, do you think he wants us to prosper?   Yes / No
(Circle correct answer.)

4. It is important in defining God's thoughts to establish them in more than one scripture. Let us examine how important it is to God that we prosper. *(Fill in the five missing words in the following scripture.)*

*"Beloved, _____ _____ _____ _____ _____ that thou mayest **prosper** and be in health, even as thy soul **prospereth**."*
(3 John 1:2 KJV)

5. From the five missing words above, what are the three words that describe how important it is to God that we prosper and be in health?

_____ _____ _____

6. It is extraordinary to consider how important this subject is to God our Father. As we saw in Psalm 35 above, we have been asked by God to say something 'continually.' What should we be saying continually? " _____

_____ _____ _____ _____, _____

_____ _____ _____ _____ _____

_____ _____ _____ _____

_____ _____ _____." *(Fill in the missing words.)*
(Psalm 35:27b KJV)

The reason we should be saying something continually, is so that we can get the revelation deep into our spirit and believe the words that are being said. By doing this we are planting a seed into our souls that will bear fruit, if we continue in it.

Make a commitment to saying Psalm 35:27 verse continually.

---

7. As we try to progress in the study of prosperity we will find there are some that do not want us to do this. This group of people will profess to be religious, but do not enter into the Kingdom of God themselves, and try to hinder others from entering. *(Fill in the four missing words in the scripture below.)*

"Woe to you lawyers! For you have taken away _____ _____ _____ _____. You did not enter in yourselves, and those who were entering in you hindered."
(Luke 11:52 NKJV)

Entering the Promises of God's Kingdom

8. What is it that we use to enter the promises of God's Kingdom? *(Luke 11:52 NKJV)* _____ _____ _____ _____.

Provisions Made for the Prosperity of Jesus

9. Let us see how God provided for the upkeep of his son Jesus. Having asked Mary to bear the child, he did not expect her and Joseph to bear the costs of providing for Jesus.

> " And when they were come into the house, they saw the young child with Mary his mother, and fell down, and worshipped him: and when they had opened their treasures, they presented unto him gifts; **gold,** and frankincense, and myrrh. "
> **(Matthew 2:11 KJV)**

10. In January 2011, gold was worth $1,416 per ounce, the weight of a typical gold coin. How many coins do you think the wise men gave in total, out of their treasures, to Joseph and Mary? _____
(We know of course that it may not have been coins, but I am using that example to see the value of what was given.)

11. How much is gold worth today per ounce? _____

12. Now by multiplying the number of estimated coins with the value of one coin we can see how great that gift was and that Jesus was indeed well provided for. So why do people say that Jesus was poor? Jesus was rich and made a sacrifice for us. Let us use the Key of Knowledge, the scriptures which enlighten us. *(Fill in the four missing words in the scripture below.)*

> "For ye know the grace of our Lord Jesus Christ, that, _____ _____ _____ _____, yet for your sakes he became poor, that ye through his poverty might be rich."
> **(II Corinthians 8:9 KJV)**

Jesus' Sacrifice

13. What happened when He made that sacrifice for us and was slain? *(Fill in the two missing words in the scripture below.)*

> "Saying with a loud voice, Worthy is the Lamb that was slain to receive power, _____ _____, and wisdom, and strength, and honour, and glory, and blessing."
> **(Revelation 5:12 KJV)**

14. In addition to receiving power, wisdom, strength, honor, glory and blessing, what else did He receive? _____

15. Jesus died so that we could have life. But do you think in going to death He stayed there? No, He was raised from the dead. Likewise, in becoming poor at the cross, Jesus received His wealth back, and He received even more when He was raised from the dead. *(Fill in the four missing words below.)*

> 4 *"But Judas Iscariot, one of his disciples (he who was about to betray him), said,*
> 5 *"Why was this ointment not sold for three hundred denarii and given to the poor?"*
> 6 *He said this, not because he cared about the poor, but because____ _____ ___ _____, and having charge of the moneybag he used to help himself to what was put into it."*
> **(John 12:4-6 ESV)**

16. What type of person did Jesus put in charge of the moneybag? _____
_____

17. Fancy having so much provision that you can afford to put a thief in charge of the money! We have seen that God has pleasure in our prosperity, and noted that it is a high priority to Him. His provision to Jesus was such that a thief could look after the money and there was still sufficiency for good works. So why is every believer not moving in prosperity? *(Fill in the five missing words below.)*

> " *Beloved, I wish above all things that thou mayest prosper and be in health, _____ ____ _____ _____ _____ ".*
>
> **(3 John 1:2 KJV)**

> Here we see that God is like any other father. He wants His children to prosper physically in proportion to the prosperity of their souls. God does not give prosperity to spiritual babies, but He does so as they mature spiritually. You would not give a car to a three-year-old, and you would not give a child everything it said it wanted. God has set it in order that our souls must prosper first, and then we prosper physically in proportion to the prosperity that is experienced by our souls. The Father does not want spoiled children.

18. Why, then, does teaching on prosperity get knocked around so much in some Christian quarters? I believe the answer can be found in the Book of Zechariah:

*Thus saith the Lord of hosts; My cities **through prosperity shall yet be spread abroad**; and the Lord shall yet comfort Zion, and shall yet choose Jerusalem."*
(Zechariah 1:17 KJV)

Reflections
1. What does God receive when we prosper?
2. How important is it to God that we prosper, and what else is equally important?
3. What should we be saying continually?
4. What do we use to enter the promises of God's Kingdom?
5. When did Jesus become poor?
6. Why did He become poor?
7. Why is it that every believer is not walking in prosperity?
8. Why is it important for Christians to prosper?

Applications
Our enemy does not want Christians to have power and wealth. We must be careful to understand that prosperity does not mean greed! Prosperity and greed are two different words. Prosperity provides the means to spread the Gospel of Jesus Christ across the world. "***My cities through prosperity shall yet be spread abroad.***"

Every Bible, every mission field, every airplane ticket, and every hall that is booked requires money! Every preacher and every preacher's family needs money! Every church and hospital that must be built requires funding! Every radio and TV broadcast costs money!

We cannot buy souls, but we can give our money to help them hear the Word.

Let us, for goodness' sake, get our heads out of the sand and see that God has provided a way for us to spread the Gospel of Jesus Christ to every city in the world.

> *"But thou shalt remember the Lord thy God: for it is he that giveth thee power to get wealth, that he may establish his covenant which he sware unto thy fathers, as it is this day."*
> ***(Deuteronomy 8:18 KJV)***

Memory Verses

"Let them shout for joy, and be glad, that favour my righteous cause: yea, let them say continually, Let the Lord be magnified, which hath pleasure in the prosperity of his servant."
(Psalm 35:27 KJV)

"Beloved, I wish above all things that thou mayest prosper and be in health, even as thy soul prospereth."
(3 John 1:2 KJV)

Closing Prayer

Father, I thank you that you want me to prosper and be in good health. I ask that you would prosper my soul that I can be a child that you are pleased with and that I can be useful for building your Kingdom. Please give me the wisdom to understand, to receive and to remember the keys needed to receive your promises. I ask these things in the name of Jesus. Amen.

Learning from the Patriarchs
Chapter Two – Study Guide

Opening Prayer

    Dear Father, thank you for giving us the Patriarchs. I ask sincerely that you would help me to learn from their lives. How you loved them, prospered them, and gave them as gifts to your body. Give me an attentive mind that I may fully digest the revelation from their lives. I ask for this in the name of Jesus. Amen.

The following questions will be answered during study of this chapter:
1. What are the two keys to poverty?
2. What are the three requirements needed to inherit the promises given to us through Abraham?
3. What are the different keys to prosperity that each of the patriarchs we studied teach?

The Patriarchs
ADAM

1. We can learn from the mistakes and success of the Patriarchs. What can we learn from Adam?

> *"And unto Adam he said, Because thou hast hearkened unto the voice of thy wife, and hast eaten of the tree, of which I commanded thee, saying, Thou shalt not eat of it: **cursed is the ground** for thy sake; **in sorrow shalt thou eat of it all the days of thy life;** Thorns also and thistles shall it bring forth to thee; and thou shalt eat the herb of the field; **In the sweat of thy face shalt thou eat bread, till thou return unto the ground;"***
> ***(Genesis 3:17-19 KJV)***

2. What did God ask Adam not to do? _____

_____

_____

3. What did Adam do? _____

Keys to Poverty

4. What is the first **Key to Poverty**? _____

5. What were the consequences for Adams actions? _____

_____

_____

_____

NOAH

6. Why was Noah given grace so that he and the few others were spared the destruction of the flood?

> *"These are the generations of Noah: **Noah was a_____ man and perfect** in his generations, and Noah _____ _____ God."*
> **(Genesis 6:9 KJV)**

> *"And Noah _____ according unto all that the LORD commanded him."*
> **(Genesis 7:5 KJV)**

7. What are the two qualities that Noah possessed that pleased God?

_____

_____

8. In the accounts of Noah we also find the second Key to Poverty? (*Read Genesis 9:20-28 and Deuteronomy 5:16.*)

What is the second **Key to Poverty**? _____

Keys to Prosperity

ABRAHAM

> *1"Now the Lord had said unto Abram, Get thee out of thy country, and from thy kindred, and from thy father's house, unto a land that I will shew thee:*
> *2 And I will make of thee a great nation, and I will bless thee, and make thy name great; and thou shalt be a blessing:*
> *3 And I will bless them that bless thee, and curse him that curseth thee: and in thee shall all families of the earth be blessed.*

*4 So Abram departed, **as the Lord had spoken unto him**; and Lot went with him: and Abram was seventy and five years old when he departed out of Haran."*
(Genesis 12:1-4 KJV)

9. What did the LORD ask Abram to do? _____

_____

10. What did the LORD promise Abram if he obeyed? _____

_____
_____
_____
_____

11. What did Abram do? _____

_____

*"And Abram went up out of Egypt, he, and his wife, and all that he had, and Lot with him, into the south. And Abram was _____ **rich** in cattle, in silver, and in gold."*
(Genesis 13:1-2 KJV)

12. After Abraham obeyed the LORD was he blessed in return? _____

13. From *Genesis 13:1-2*, how rich did Abram become? _____

_____

14. What is the Key to Prosperity that can be found in Abraham's life?

_____

> *All the blessings that came upon Abraham, the blessings that came upon his descendants, and the blessings that came to all nations were because Abraham believed and obeyed God's voice. When one wants to do anything for God, you must **listen to** and **obey** His voice.*

ISAAC

"And God said, Sarah thy wife shall bear thee a son indeed; and thou shalt call his name Isaac: and I will establish my covenant with him for an everlasting covenant, and with his seed after him."
(Genesis 17:19 KJV)

2 "And the Lord appeared unto him, and said, Go not down into Egypt; dwell in the land which I shall tell thee of:
*3 Sojourn in this land, and **I will be with thee, and will bless thee;** for unto thee, and unto thy seed, I will give all these countries, and I will perform the oath which I sware unto Abraham thy father;*
4 And I will make thy seed to multiply as the stars of heaven, and will give unto thy seed all these countries; and in thy seed shall all the nations of the earth be blessed;
*5 **Because that** _____ _____ _____ _____,*
and kept my charge, my commandments, my statutes, and my laws."
(Genesis 26:2-5 KJV)

"And _____ _____ _____ _____, then are ye Abraham's seed, and heirs according to the promise."
(Galatians 3:29 KJV)

15. What is the condition by which we can be heirs of the promise given to Abraham? _____

16. What are the three requirements we need to obtain the promises found in *Hebrews 6:12?*
   1 _____
   2 _____
   3 _____

17. Examine how God prospered Isaac. What is the key to prosperity found in Isaac's life? _____

"And Abraham _____ all that he had unto Isaac."
(Genesis 25:5 KJV)

Isaac received the blessing because of his father, Abraham. It was not by his own efforts that he was blessed. He received the blessing as an inheritance. Because of the death of Jesus, we have inherited the promises that came to Jesus through Abraham and Isaac.

JACOB

18. Life was not easy for Jacob. Indeed, he was the holder of the promises that were given to Abraham and Isaac, yet there was quite a long waiting period before he received them. Jacob worked very hard for his father in law Laban. How many years did Jacob work for Laban? _____

> 38 "This twenty years have I been with thee; thy ewes and thy she goats have not cast their young, and the rams of thy flock have I not eaten.
> 39 That which was torn of beasts I brought not unto thee; I bare the loss of it; of my hand didst thou require it, whether stolen by day, or stolen by night.
> 40 Thus I was; in the day the drought consumed me, and the frost by night; and my sleep departed from mine eyes.
> 41 Thus have I been twenty years in thy house; I served thee fourteen years for thy two daughters, and six years for thy cattle: and thou hast changed my wages ten times.
> 42 Except the God of my father, the God of Abraham, and the fear of Isaac, had been with me, surely thou hadst sent me away now empty. God hath seen mine affliction and the labour of my hands, and rebuked thee yesternight."
> **(Genesis 31:38-42 KJV)**

19. What two things did God see, whilst Jacob worked for Laban?

　　1. _____

　　2. _____

20. What qualities are the keys to prosperity which we learn from Jacob's life?

　　1. _____

　　2. _____

　　This long period of work for Jacob was not easy. Laban was not a good employer, as was evidenced by him changing Jacob's wages ten times and requiring him to replace damaged and stolen goods. These would be hard terms for a stranger, let alone for your own son-in-law! He went through drought, frost, and sleeplessness. It was not an easy time.

　　Sometimes, as Christians, we can look at the promises and inheritance so much that we forget that hard work is sometimes also required. Jacob went through affliction and labor for twenty years! This is why the Scripture says that it is through faith and patience that we inherit the promises of God. (See Hebrews 6:12.)

The promises are true,
but sometimes we have to labor.
Do not be surprised.

Wrestling With God!

21. What did Jacob say to God? _____

_____

> 24 *"And Jacob was left alone; and there wrestled a man with him until the breaking of the day.*
>
> 25 *And when he saw that he prevailed not against him, he touched the hollow of his thigh; and the hollow of Jacob's thigh was out of joint, as he wrestled with him.*
>
> 26 *And he said, Let me go, for the day breaketh. And he said, ___*
> *_____ _____ _____ _____ _____, _____*
> *_____ _____ _____.*
>
> 27 *And he said unto him, What is thy name? And he said, Jacob.*
>
> 28 *And he said, Thy name shall be called no more Jacob, but Israel: for as a prince hast thou power with God and with men, and hast prevailed.*
>
> 29 *And Jacob asked him, and said, Tell me, I pray thee, thy name. And he said, Wherefore is it that thou dost ask after my name?* **And he_____ him there."**
>
> **(Genesis 32: 24-29 KJV)**

22. What did God do? He _____ him there.

23. Here we see Jacob's attitude toward God. He would not let God go until he was blessed. This attitude pleased God. Likewise, when the Canaanite woman spoke to Jesus for the healing of her daughter, she was not put off by Jesus' protestations that He would not help. She knew that God would help. Was her daughter healed? _____

> 22 *"And, behold, a woman of Canaan came out of the same coasts, and cried unto him, saying, Have mercy on me, O Lord, thou Son of David; my daughter is grievously vexed with a devil.*
>
> 23 *But he answered her not a word. And his disciples came and besought him, saying, Send her away; for she crieth after us.*
>
> 24 *But he answered and said, I am not sent but unto the lost sheep of the house of Israel.*
>
> 25 *Then came she and worshipped him, saying, Lord, help me.*
>
> 26 *But he answered and said, It is not meet to take the children's bread, and to cast it to dogs.*
>
> 27 *And she said, Truth, Lord: yet the dogs eat of the crumbs which fall from their masters' table.*
>
> 28 *Then Jesus answered and said unto her, O woman, great is thy faith: be it unto thee even as thou wilt. And her daughter was made whole from that very hour."*
>
> **(Matthew 15:22-28 KJV)**

This woman persevered until she received from Jesus what she needed. Jesus acknowledged how great her faith was in light of her determination.

If you truly, truly know that God will bless you, then you will not let Him go. When you don't really believe, then you won't pray much at all.

This attitude of Jacob is described in the Psalms:

> " This is the generation of them _____ _____ _____, that seek _____ _____, O Jacob. Selah."
> **(Psalm 24:6 KJV)**

God likes intimacy with us, but He won't force us to come close to Him. We have to desire to draw close to Him and seek His face. Let us have eyes to see. Intimacy with God and prayer to Him are vital keys to prosperity.

JOSEPH

In Joseph's life we see what appears to be many contradictions. Instead of blessing and prosperity, we see anguish, suffering, toil, and affliction. Surely, also we should see prosperity, not affliction in his life.

It is sometimes hard to understand the relationship between our inheritance of prosperity from God and the times when we are called into suffering and poverty.

As we follow the account of Joseph, we see that his enormous change of circumstances was for a purpose—the saving of the whole world. We see the outcome that God had put in place for him!

> *"And God sent me before you to preserve you a posterity in the earth, and to save your lives by a great deliverance."*
> **(Genesis 45:7 KJV)**

We can also see this laying aside of our rights in the life of Jesus:

> 6 *"Who, being in the form of God, thought it not robbery to be equal with God:*
> 7 **But made himself of no reputation, and took upon him the _____ of a_____, and was made in the likeness of men:**
> 8 *And being found in fashion as a man, he humbled himself, and _____ _____ unto death, even the* death of the cross."
> **(Philippians 2:6-8 KJV)**

> *"For ye know the grace of our Lord Jesus Christ, that, though he was rich,* **yet for your sakes he became poor,** *that ye through his poverty might be rich."*
> **(2 Corinthians 8:9 KJV)**

As it says in Ecclesiastes, "Better is the end of a thing than the beginning thereof." *(See Ecclesiastes 7:8 KJV).*

When Jesus, the King of kings and Lord of lords, came to earth, He was stripped of His majesty. For the purposes of God He was obedient unto the death of the cross, and because of His obedience, He was highly exalted, and given a name above all names.

In the continuing account of Joseph's life (*39th Chapter of Genesis*), we see him being trained for the job that was ahead of him. Through difficult times, the **careful positioning** of his circumstances brought him to the fulfillment of his life's purpose: the saving of the world.

I think it is quite poignant that Joseph named his first two children Manasseh and Ephraim.

Manasseh: For God said he hath made me forget all my toil.

Ephraim: For God hath caused me to be fruitful in the land of my affliction.

> *When you put the meaning of the two names of Manasseh and Ephraim together, we learn: "God has made me forget all my toil and caused me to be fruitful in the land of my affliction." It is quite clear from the account of Joseph's life that it was for the purposes of God that he went through that "land of affliction." It is also quite clear that a "season of fruitfulness" follows such times.*

24. Each of the patriarchs teaches us a different key to prosperity. What are they?

Noah - _____

Abraham - _____

Isaac - _____

Jacob - _____

Joseph - _____

Reflections
1. What is the first key to poverty?
2. What is the second key to poverty?
3. What are the three requirements needed to inherit the promises given to us through Abraham?

Applications
Ask the Holy Spirit to reveal any uncleanness, disobedience, laziness, and/or selfishness within your heart. Confess and repent of these things and then ask again.

Memory Verses
"That ye be not slothful, but followers of them who through faith and patience inherit the promises."
(Hebrews 6:12 KJV)

"And if ye be Christ's, then are ye Abraham's seed, and heirs according to the promise."
(Galatians 3:29 KJV)

Closing Prayer

Dear Father: I thank you that you prospered each of the Patriarchs. You prospered Noah because of righteousness. I thank you that I am the righteousness of God in Jesus. Please help me to cleanse myself from all filthiness of the flesh and spirit, perfecting holiness. (*See I Corinthians 7:1*) I ask this in Jesus' name.

Father, you asked Abraham to obey you. Please teach me to be obedient and listen to your heavenly voice. I ask this in Jesus' name.

I thank you that you prospered Isaac through inheritance. I thank you that Jesus died for me and that I receive the promises given to Abraham through Jesus.

I thank you that you prospered Jacob through hard work. Teach my hands to be diligent, that I may be a son (or daughter) that pleases you.

Father, you prospered Joseph and Jesus through their sacrifices. LORD, I ask that you would give me a heart that I would lay my life down for my friends. I ask this in the name of Jesus. Amen.

Prosperity of the Kings
Chapter Three – Study Guide

Opening Prayer

Dear Father who art in Heaven, please open my eyes and heart to understand the majesty you gave to the Kings of Israel and Judah. Please help me to learn from their successes and failures. I ask this in the name of Jesus. Amen.

The following questions will be answered during study of this chapter:

1. What was the average reign of a King whose reign was righteous?
2. What was the average reign of a King whose reign was evil?
3. What did Solomon ask God for?
4. What stood out in David's relationship with the LORD?
5. What happened when the Kings sought the LORD?

Lessons To Be Learned

In our study of prosperity we can look at the kings of Israel and Judah for additional insights. When they listened and served God, He gave them length of days and prosperity. When they did not listen, they perished early.

> *"But with kings on the throne he sets them forever, and they are exalted...**If they listen and serve him, they complete their days in prosperity,** and their years in pleasantness. **But if they do not listen, they perish by the sword and die without knowledge."***
> *(Job 36:7b-11 NASV)*

1. What happens to a King that listens and serves God? _____

_____

2. What happens to a King that doesn't listen? _____

_____

3. Solomon offered a thousand burnt offerings on that altar. At Gibeon the LORD appeared to Solomon in a dream by night; and God said, "Ask! What shall I give you?" What did Solomon say?

" Give to Your servant an _____ _____ to judge Your people, that I may discern between good and evil. For who is able to judge this great people of Yours?"
(1 Kings 3:9 NKJV)

3."And Solomon loved the Lord, walking in the statutes of his father David, except that he sacrificed and burned incense at the high places.
4 Now the king went to Gibeon to sacrifice there, for that was the great high place: Solomon offered a thousand burnt offerings on that altar.
5 At Gibeon the Lord appeared to Solomon in a dream by night; and God said, "Ask! What shall I give you?"
6 And Solomon said: "You have shown great mercy to Your servant David my father, because he walked before You in truth, in righteousness, and in uprightness of heart with You; You have continued this great kindness for him, and You have given him a son to sit on his throne, as it is this day.
7 Now, O Lord my God, You have made Your servant king instead of my father David, but I am a little child; I do not know how to go out or come in.
8 And Your servant is in the midst of Your people whom You have chosen, a great people, too numerous to be numbered or counted.
9 Therefore give to Your servant an understanding heart to judge Your people, that I may discern between good and evil. For who is able to judge this great people of Yours?"
10 The speech pleased the Lord, that Solomon had asked this thing.
11Then God said to him: "Because you have asked this thing, and have not asked long life for yourself, nor have asked riches for yourself, nor have asked the life of your enemies, but have asked for yourself understanding to discern justice,
12 Behold, I have done according to your words; see, I have given you a wise and understanding heart, so that there has not been anyone like you before you, nor shall any like you arise after you.
13 And I have also given you what you have not asked: both _____and _____, so that there shall not be anyone like you among the kings all your days.
14 So if you walk in My ways, to keep My statutes and My commandments, as your father David walked, then I will lengthen your days."
(1 Kings 3:3-14 NKJV)

4. In addition to an understanding heart what two things did God also give to Solomon?

    1. _____

    2. _____

5. God will always respond to requests for provisions to build His kingdom. Not only did God give Solomon wisdom, but He also gave him what he did not ask for. What truth of these verses is reflected in *3 John*?

"Beloved, I wish above all things that thou mayest prosper and be in health, _____ as thy soul _____."
(3 John 1:2 KJV)

God desires us to prosper and have a long life. Yet, more important to Him is the prospering of our souls. Solomon showed maturity (the prospering of his soul) in desiring an understanding heart for God's people. Then God responded with riches and honor. If we view being a Christian as a means to gain money, things, and possessions, we are showing great immaturity. If we see prospering as an opportunity for the gospel to advance, then we are getting closer to being the child that God desires.

Apart from the great wealth of David and the immense riches of Solomon, we do not find a great deal with regard to the wealth of the other kings. As there is a correlation between God's blessings of wealth and long life, we may look at the length of their reigns to give us an indication of God's response to them.

By making a list of the kings who did evil and the kings who did right, we find an astonishing difference in the relative lengths of their reigns.

The average reign of a king who did right was 30.01 years. The average reign of a king who did evil, on the other hand, was 2.81 years!

Kings That Did Evil

Jehoram	8 years
Jehoiachin	0.25 years
Zachariah	0.5 years
Jehoash	16 years
Jeroboam	41 years
Pekah	20 years
Menahem	10 years
Eliakim, changed to Jehoiakim	11 years
Hoshea	9 years
Amon	2 years
Jehoahaz	0.25 years
Ahaz	10 years
Jehoahaz	17 years
Mattaniah, changed to Zedekiah	11 years
Baasha	24 years
Abijam or Abijah	3 years
Nadab	2 years
Ahaziah	2 years
Jehoram (Joram)	12 years
Ahaziah	1 year
Pekahiah	2 years

Omri	12 years
Jeroboam	22 years
Elah	2 years
Zimri	0.02 years
Ahab	22 years

Kings That Did Righteously

David	40 years
Jehoshaphat	25 years
Jehoash (Joash)	40 years
Jotham	16 years
Josiah	31 years
Amaziah	29 years
Hezekiah	29 years
Azariah (Uzziah)	52 years
Asa	41 years
Jehu	28 years

Below are some interesting verses in reference to the kings' relationships with God. All of the kings are not included, but only some relevant verses that can help us understand how God works.

> *"So **David inquired of the Lord, saying**, "Shall I go up against the Philistines? Will You deliver them into my hand?" **And the Lord said to David**, "Go up, for I will doubtless deliver the Philistines into your hand."*
> *(2 Samuel 5:19 NKJV)*

The great King David, after whom I named my son, became great because God was with him. His reign was marked by the various times when he inquired of the Lord. David did not make these inquiries to God in order to receive from Him; on the contrary, David drew close to God in order to obey Him. Saul wanted information and guidance from God, but David wanted an intimate and personal relationship with Him.

KING JEROBOAM

In the New Testament, Paul tells us to "set our minds on things above not on things on the earth." *(See Colossians 3:2 NKJV)*

> *26 And Jeroboam said in his heart, Now shall the kingdom return to the house of David:*
> *27 If this people go up to do sacrifice in the house of the Lord at Jerusalem, then shall the heart of this people turn again unto their lord, even unto Rehoboam king of Judah, and they shall kill me, and go again to Rehoboam king of Judah.*

28 Whereupon the king took counsel, and made two calves of gold, and said unto them, It is too much for you to go up to Jerusalem: behold thy gods, O Israel, which brought thee up out of the land of Egypt.
29 And he set the one in Bethel, and the other put he in Dan.
30 And this thing became a sin: for the people went to worship before the one, even unto Dan.
(1 Kings 12:26-31 KJV)

6. How did Jeroboam try to solve his political problems and fears?

_____

_____

Jeroboam should have inquired of the Lord with regard to how to solve this problem. The advice he received from his worldly advisors worked in a way on the earthly plane, but it was so far from the mark on the heavenly plane.

7 "Because I exalted you from among the people and made you leader over My people Israel,
8 and tore the kingdom away from the house of David and gave it to you — yet you have not been like My servant David, who kept My commandments and who followed Me with all his heart, to do only that which was right in My sight;
9 you also have done more evil than all who were before you, and have gone and made for yourself other gods and molten images to provoke Me to anger, and have cast Me behind your back —
10 therefore behold, I am bringing calamity on the house of Jeroboam, and will cut off from Jeroboam every male person, both bond and free in Israel, and I will make a clean sweep of the house of Jeroboam, as one sweeps away dung until it is all gone."
(1 Kings 14:7b-10 NASV)

Unlike King David, Jeroboam was earthly minded, and he lost everything for himself and his family.

KING REHOBOAM

Rehoboam's reign is marked by the exchange of the gold shields for bronze shields. This reveals a fading of the glory.

Under David and Solomon the Kingdom of Israel was a glorious kingdom, but then it began to fade. In fact, it was split into two, with Israel under Jeroboam and Judah under Rehoboam. Yet, in Rehoboam's reign we see the glory fading away.

7. Why was the glory fading away? What can we learn from Rehoboam's relationship with God that has caused this fading away, and what can we learn from the fading away, as well?

25 "Now it happened in the fifth year of King Rehoboam, that Shishak the king of Egypt came up against Jerusalem.
*26 He took away the treasures of the house of the Lord and the treasures of the king's house, and he took everything, even taking **all the shields of gold** which Solomon had made*
*27 So King Rehoboam **made shields of bronze** in their place, ..."*
(I Kings 14:25-27 NASV)

"Thus saith the Lord, "_____ _____ _____ _____ ,
and therefore have I also left you in the hand of Shishak."
(2 Chronicles 12:5b KJV)

8. What did King Rehoboam do, for God to leave him in the hand of Shishak? _____
_____

" And he did evil, because he _____ not his _____ to seek the Lord." .
(2 Chronicles 12:14 KJV)

9. What did King Rehoboam NOT do? _____
_____

If we begin to rest on our laurels, we may see the glory fade away. It may start with a little less prayer, fewer quiet times, or not seeking the Lord as much as we did previously. It is quite easy to fade away. One can see from Rehoboam's life *(See 2 Chronicles 12:14)* that he did evil because he was not prepared to seek the Lord. That was the beginning of downfall for him. It was an absence of preparation, because his life had now been established.

Unlike his grandfather David who was always seeking the Lord, Rehoboam stopped doing so and was then humbled by Shishak, the King of Egypt. When one stops seeking God, stops reading His law (His Word), then one finds a law that says that evil is always present and waiting at the door.

The absence of God will always allow the opportunity for the presence of evil. We can also see from Rehoboam's life that he humbled himself and repented after God sent his prophet to him. We also can see that God relented and did not destroy them. So there is always hope! People need to make sure they humble themselves and repent, so God can change their glory from bronze to gold again.

One needs to repent of sin. Remember, all people have sinned and fallen short of the glory of God. *(See Romans 3:23)*. The glory in our lives is the

Presence of God within, radiating out. Let that radiance be gold, not bronze.

From the Scriptures above we can see that when Rehoboam's kingdom was established, it was then that he forsook the law of the LORD, with the result that he sinned; then God allowed the King of Egypt to come against him.

God has many friends when people are trying to establish themselves in Him. How frequent are their prayers at this time. Yet, when many people are established, they find themselves in a comfort zone. It seems that their comfort zone tests their hearts. In light of this, what will they do when they become successful?

> 1 "And it came to pass, **when Rehoboam had established the kingdom**, and had strengthened himself, **he forsook the law of the Lord**, and all Israel with him.
> 2 And it came to pass, that in the fifth year of king Rehoboam Shishak king of Egypt came up against Jerusalem, **because they had transgressed against the Lord.**"
> **(2 Chronicles 12:1-2 KJV)**

KING HEZEKIAH

In the life of King Hezekiah we have a wonderful example of how God blesses us. Hezekiah cleaved, departed not, followed, and kept God's commandments. As a result, the LORD was with him and he prospered wherever he went.

> 5 "He _____ in the Lord God of Israel; so that after him was none like him among all the kings of Judah, nor **any** that were before him.
> 6 For he _____ to the Lord, **and** _____ _____
> from following him, but _____ his commandments, which the Lord commanded Moses.
> 7 And the Lord was with him; **and** he prospered whithersoever he went forth:...".
> **(2 Kings 18:5-7a KJV)**

KING ASA

King Asa built and prospered while he was seeking God with all his heart. Therefore, he experienced an incredible victory against the Ethiopians. *(See 2 Chronicles. 14:2-12 NKJV)*

Although King Asa did not go over to other gods, he did start relying more on men than he did on God. He relied on Ben-Hadad of Syria for deliverance, and he relied on physicians to cure his diseased feet. The outcome of these changes was that the Prophet Hanani gave this word: "From now on you shall have wars." *(See 2 Chronicles16:7-14 NKJV)*

When King Asa sought the Lord with all his heart, he was given peace; in that God-given peace he was able to build. However, when King Asa

sought help from men, he was given wars. In war it is hard to build because all of your attention must go to the battles.

If we look at plants and animals, we can see that they start small (as a tiny seed) and then they begin to grow.

Let us examine our lives. Are we growing, prospering, and building? Or are we continually fighting problems (wars)? Are we moving ahead, or are we going nowhere?

King David was continually seeking the Lord. He ran his race and won. If you have gotten off track by distractions, this is a good time to repent and seek the Lord's face.

KING JEHOSHAPHAT

King Jehoshaphat sought God as David his forefather had done. Because he did so, God was with him, he had peace, and he was able to build. He became increasingly powerful with great riches and honor. Even his enemies gave tribute to him. *(See 2 Chronicles 17:3-12 NKJV)*

The only blemish that can be found in Jehospaphats' reign was that he joined with Ahaziah, King of Israel, for a business venture. They built a fleet of ships to go trading to Tarshish. But God destroyed them. *(See 2 Chronicles 20:35-37.)*

> *"Do not be _____ yoked with _____. For what partnership has righteousness with lawlessness? Or what fellowship has light with darkness?"*
> **(2 Corinthians 6:14 ESV)**

Traditionally we use this verse in reference to marriage to unbelievers. But equally I think we have to be just as careful about being joined to unbelievers in business ventures. How can two walk together unless they be agreed? *(See Amos 3:3.)*

KING UZZIAH

3 "Sixteen years old was Uzziah when he began to reign, and he reigned fifty and two years in Jerusalem. His mother's name also was Jecoliah of Jerusalem.

*4 And he did **that which** was right in the sight of the LORD, according to all that his father Amaziah did.*
*5 And he sought God in the days of Zechariah, who had understanding in the visions of God: **and as long as he sought the LORD,** God made him to prosper.*
(2 Chronicles 26:3-5 KJV)

The understanding we gain from looking at all the relationships these kings had with God can be summed up as follows:

---

and as long as he sought the LORD,
God made him to prosper.
(2 Chronicles 26:3-5 KJV)

Reflections

1. What was the average reign of a King who acted righteously?
2. What was the average reign of a King who acted evil?
3. What did Solomon ask God for?
4. What stood out in David's relationship with the LORD?
5. What happened when the Kings sought the LORD?

Applications

Enquire of the Lord if there is anything he wants you to do. Write it down.

Memory Verses

"...and as long as he sought the Lord, God made him to prosper."
(2 Chronicles 26:5b KJV)

"So David inquired of the Lord, saying, "Shall I go up against the Philistines? Will You deliver them into my hand?..."
(2 Samuel 5:19a NKJV)

Closing Prayer

Dear Father, I ask that you would give to me an understanding heart to discern between good and evil, as you gave to King Solomon. I ask that you would always enquire of you, as did your servant King David. Let my mind be set on things above and no on earth below. I ask this in the name of Jesus. Amen.

MONEY
Chapter Four – Study Guide

Opening Prayer
    Dear Father, please help me to understand money, how to use it for your Kingdom, and not worship the God of Mammon. I ask this in the name of Jesus. Amen.

The following questions will be answered during study of this chapter:
1. What is the root of all evil?
2. What is money?
3. What is the translation of the word money in Genesis?

Root of Money
    "For _____ _____ _____ _____ is the root of all evil."
(1 Timothy 6:10 KJV)

1. What is the root of all evil? _____ _____ _____ _____

This has often been misquoted as, "Money is the root of all evil."

Yes, it is the love of the money which is the root of all evil, not the money itself. If money were the root of all evil, we could say that God was evil in giving money to Abraham, Isaac, Jacob, Joseph, Solomon, etc. God is never the author of evil, though. So of course money is not evil. But what is money?

What Is Money?
From Genesis we see that the word translated as "money" is כֶּסֶף, pronounced *keceph,* which means *"silver."* In conjunction with the word for silver or gold, we have the words gerahs, shekels, and talents, which were used as measurements of weight, thus giving an exact measurement of worth. The money could be a shekel of silver or a shekel of gold, etc. The value was in the amount of gold or silver that was used to make the coin.

We see, then, that with accurate measurements of weight and value, goods and services could be bought and sold for these coins, thereby providing a commercial standard to work with.

As civilization advanced, the value of money changed from the value of the coins themselves to paper money and metal coins, with the value being shown as a promise from the issuing body.

For example, English paper money has a promise from the Bank of England to pay the bearer on demand the number of pounds stated on the note. This is signed by the Chief Cashier ". . . for the Governor and Company of the Bank of England." The value of the note is more than the paper it is printed on; the value is in the power of the promise from the Bank of England.

It is interesting to read what Jesus said when He was questioned about whether people should pay tribute unto Caesar or not:

> 21 *"And they asked him,...*
> 22 *'Is is lawful for us to give tribute unto Caesar, or no?'*
> 23 *But he perceived their craftiness, and said unto them, 'Why tempt ye me?*
> 24 *Show me a penny. Whose image and superscription hath it?' They answered and said, 'Caesar's.'*
> 25 *And he said unto them, 'Render therefore unto Caesar the things which be Caesar's and unto God the things which be God's'."*
> **(Luke 21:25 KJV)**

2. Who made this money? _____

The coin translated as "a penny" was a Roman *denarius*, Jesus recognized that this piece of money was Caesar's. The power given in the money had come from Caesar.

With all modern currencies the power invested in them can be traced back to their originators. This is why we get fluctuations in currency prices as the powers behind the notes change! We see differences between strong currencies and weak currencies. Currency from Western countries, such as U.S. dollars and UK pounds sterling do not change a great deal in value unless economic conditions warrant such changes. However, currencies from third-world countries and countries at war can fluctuate greatly. These currencies can even end up with no value at all! This is because the value of these currencies is in the power and promises behind them.

In this time we are seeing the representation of the power invested in money being registered more and more in electronic form. Money is moved from one account to another electronically through computers. Often, physical money is not exchanged, because goods are paid for electronically through credit cards.

Even so, the money still represents the power that is behind it. This is true whether it is held in pounds sterling, U.S. dollars, or any other standard.

If there is a complete financial collapse these currencies and the power behind them could be worth nothing. They would only be worth the paper they are written on. *It is well worth having a proportion of your financial worth in hard assets like gold and silver.*

We know from the *Book of Revelation* that there will come a time when people will not be able to buy or sell without the name or mark or number of the beast.

Let us not forget that this is not determined by how the money is transmitted, physically, electronically, etc., but it is a reflection of the power and authority of the beast behind that particular type of money. Eternal damnation follows those who enter into that system. This will not be something that people will fall into by mistake! Let's make sure that we invest our money into the bank accounts of the Kingdom of Heaven, where moth, rust, and thieves cannot corrupt and steal.

Reflections
1. What is the root of all evil?
2. What is money?
3. What is the translation of the word "money"?
4. Does the Kingdom of Heaven have a bank account?

Memory Verse
"For the love of money is the root of all evil: which while some coveted after, they have erred from the faith, and pierced themselves through with many sorrows."
(I Timothy 6:10 KJV)

Closing Prayer
Dear Father, please help me to understand money, how to use it for your Kingdom, and not worship the God of Mammon. I ask this in the name of Jesus. Amen.

The Bank of God-Our Bank Account
Chapter Five – Study Guide

Opening Prayer

Dear Father, please help me to realize the reality of your accounts in heaven. Help me to understand it, that I may set my mind on things above, the important things, and not on things on the earth. I ask this in the name of Jesus. Amen.

The following questions will be answered during study of this chapter:
1. Where does it say in scripture that we have an account?
2. Why could Paul say that fruit was being put into the Philippians' account?
3. When we give, what type of interest do we receive in our accounts? *(See Luke 6:38 KJV)*
4. When we sow abundantly, how shall we receive?

Fruit

The Scriptures show us clearly that God has a different view of our finances than we have. For example, the Book of Revelation talks about those who are rich, yet are poor, and those who are poor, yet are rich. *(See Revelation 2:9 and 3:17 KJV)*. These passages suggest that the earthly view of our wealth may not be our correct financial position. We may think we are rich, but the truth could be that we are poor, and vice-versa.

> *15 "Now you Philippians know also that in the beginning of the gospel, when I departed from Macedonia, no church shared with me concerning giving and receiving but you only.*
> *16 For even in Thessalonica you sent aid once and again for my necessities.*
> *17 Not that I seek the gift, but **I seek the fruit that abounds to your account.**"*
> ***(Philippians 4:15-17 NKJV)***

When Paul received aid from the Philippians, he said that he did not seek the gift.

1. What did he say that he was seeking? _____

_____

Paul recognized that we have an account.

19 "Do not lay up for yourselves treasures on earth, where moth and rust destroy and where thieves break in and steal;
20 but lay up for yourselves _____ in_____,
where neither moth nor rust destroys and where thieves do not break in and steal.
21 For where your treasure is, there your heart will be also."
(Matthew 6:19 -21 NKJV)

2. Where did Jesus say we should put our treasures? _____

_____

3. Why should we put our treasure there? _____

_____

Increase

"Give, and it will be given to you: _____ measure,_____
down, _____ together, and _____ over will be
put into your bosom. For with the same measure that you use, it will be
measured back to you."
(Luke 6:38 NKJV)

4. How did Jesus say that we get our money into our heavenly bank accounts? _____

_____

5. How did He describe the 'return' we would receive on our giving?

_____

_____

As we give, it will be given back to us. It seems that God has set in order spiritual laws that prosper us when we give. O what beautiful wisdom—growth through giving; there is no room for greed in this system. A greedy man would not ever be able to give in faith.

See how this is backed up in *3 John*:

" Beloved, I wish above all things that thou mayest prosper and be in
health, _____ as thy soul prospereth."
(3 John 1:2 KJV)

6. Though God wants us to prosper financially, what else does He say He wants to prosper at the same rate? _____

Spiritual Maturity

As the child of God learns to give, the child of God prospers. This prosperity comes in proportion to one's spiritual maturity.

We now see why Jesus told the rich young man to give his money away. It is because he had no money in his bank account in Heaven! In fact, he had a lack!

> *22 So when Jesus heard these things, He said to him,* **"You** _____ _____ *one thing. Sell all that you have and distribute to the poor, and you will have treasure in heaven; and come, follow Me."*
> *23 But when he heard this, he became very sorrowful, for he was very rich.*
> *24 And when Jesus saw that he became very sorrowful, He said, "How hard it is for those who have riches to enter the kingdom of God!*
> *25 For it is easier for a camel to go through the eye of a needle than for a rich man to enter the kingdom of God."*
> **(Luke 18:22-25 NKJV)**

With God All Things Are Possible
(See Matthew 19:23-30; Mark 10:23-31)

---

7. What did Jesus say would happen after the rich young man would sell his possessions and give to the poor? _____ _____ _____ _____ _____ _____.

It is important for us not to look on the outside of a person. Though the rich young man was wealthy in the physical realm, he was not spiritually prosperous. It is better to be both!

> *14 "And to the angel of the church of the Laodiceans write, 'These things says the Amen, the Faithful and True Witness, the Beginning of the creation of God:*
> *15 "I know your works, that you are neither cold nor hot. I could wish you were cold or hot.*
> *16 So then, because you are lukewarm, and neither cold nor hot, I will vomit you out of My mouth.*
> *17 Because you say,* **'I am rich, have become wealthy, and have need of nothing' — and do not know that you are wretched, miserable, poor, blind, and naked.'"**
> **(Revelation 3:14-17 NKJV)**

The Laodiceans said that they were _____, but God said that they were _____
Sometimes we are not able to recognize our own spiritual state.

> *8 "And to the angel of the church in Smyrna write, 'These things says the First and the Last, who was dead, and came to life:*
> *9 "I know your works, tribulation, and poverty (but you are rich);"*
> **(Revelation 2:8-9a NKJV)**

In the same way it seemed that the church in Smyrna were poor, yet God said they are rich!

28 "Then Peter said, "See, we have left all and followed You."
29 So He said to them, "Assuredly, I say to you, there is no one who has left house or parents or brothers or wife or children, for the sake of the kingdom of God,
30 who shall not receive many times more _____ _____ _____ _____, and in the age to come eternal life."
(Luke 18:28-30 NKJV)

8. Did Jesus say to Peter that they would have to wait until the time to come to receive from their giving? _____

9. When did Jesus say that they would receive from their giving? _____
_____

So we can see that in order to increase the amount of money in our heavenly account, we have to give it away.

Sowing and Reaping

There is a further aspect to this: if we sow sparingly, we shall reap sparingly, and if we sow bountifully, we shall reap bountifully.

"But this I say, He which soweth sparingly shall reap also _____; and he which soweth bountifully shall reap also _____."
(2 Corinthians 9:6 KJV)

What if I don't want to reap bountifully; what if I only want enough to meet my needs?

Believe it or not, that is a selfish response, for **the reason to reap bountifully is so we can have sufficiency to meet every good work!** Who will feed the poor, who will pay for Bibles, churches, Christian radio and TV stations; who will provide for the needs of missionaries and the mission field?

If we receive according to what we give isn't that easier for the people who have more?

There are some who think it is only for the wealthy to give and not for the poor to give. That these laws are only for those who have some of this world's wealth.

31

41 "Now Jesus sat opposite the treasury and saw how the people put money into the treasury. And many who were rich put in much.
42 Then one poor widow came and threw in two mites, which make a quadrans.
43 So He called His disciples to Himself and said to them, "Assuredly, I say to you that this poor widow has put in more than all those who have given to the treasury;
*44 for they all put in out of their abundance, **but she out of her poverty but in all that she had, her whole livelihood."***
(Mark 12:41-44 NKJV)

10. Who put the most money into the treasury? _____

_____

We see here that although the poor widow only put in two mites, Jesus said she had put in more than all the rich people. With God, it is always according to what we have, not according to what we do not have. Also, when we are faithful with little, we shall be faithful with much.

So if we have an account in Heaven, then how do we make withdrawals?

1 "Cast your bread upon the waters, For you will find it _____
_____ _____.
2 Give a serving to seven, and also to eight, For you do not know what evil will be on the earth.
3 If the clouds are full of rain, They empty themselves upon the earth; *And if a tree falls to the south or the north, In the place where the tree falls, there it shall lie."*
(Ecclesiastics 11:1-3 NKJV)

11. When you cast your bread upon the waters, will you find it again? ___

_____

12. When will you find it? _____

Solomon said that we should cast our bread on the waters and give a serving to seven and eight. He is not telling us to toss our dinner in the river! Nor is he advising us to give lots of dinner parties.

Instead, he is telling us to *give*. By giving you are ensuring your future, no matter what evil may occur. "If the clouds are full of rain, they empty themselves upon the Earth."

The clouds are in the heavens. When you give your tithes and offerings, or when you give to the poor, you are filling that cloud in Heaven with rain.

Clouds full of water empty back down to the Earth. You may not know when, but they most certainly will. My own testimony about tithing proves this: in one day I had a downpour of $200,000 after earning only $5000 during the entire year before!

> *"If the clouds are full of rain,* _____ _____
> _____ _____ _____ _____ ;
> *And if a tree falls to the south or the north, In the place where the tree falls, there it shall lie."*
> **(Ecclesiastes 11:3 NKJV)**

When a tree falls to the ground, it remains where it lies because of the weight of the tree and the force of gravity. Through this image God wants us to know that the spiritual laws of receiving after giving are as strong as the universal law of gravity.

Let us now go back to *Philippians 4.*

> *16 For even in Thessalonica you sent aid once and again for my necessities.*
> *17 Not that I seek the gift, but **I seek the fruit that abounds to your account.***
> *18 Indeed I have all and abound. I am full, having received from Epaphroditus the things sent from you, a sweet-smelling aroma, an acceptable sacrifice, well pleasing to God.*
> *19 **And my God shall supply all your need according to His riches in glory by Christ Jesus."***
> **(Philippians 4:16-19 NKJV)**

Here we see a dilemma that pastors often have to face. They want their churches to prosper by giving, yet they do not want to be seen as seeking the gift. *(See Philippians 4:17 NKJV).*

We have to get rid of pride and preach the Word, even if it seems to benefit us!

> *"My God shall supply all your need according to His riches in glory by Christ Jesus."*
> **(Philippians 4:19 NKJV)**

This verse is so often abused and spoken out of context. The reason Paul could so confidently pronounce that God was going to supply all their need according to His riches in glory by Christ Jesus, was because they had just given once and again to him!

Don't think that you will obtain these things from God just by speaking the verse. It does not come by simply confessing the verse; first, you have to give! This is exactly what the Philippians had done.

"He who has pity on the poor _____ _____ _____
_____, And He will pay back what he has given."
(Proverbs 19:17 NKJV)

13. When you give to the poor, who are you lending to? _____

If you are lending your money, then you will receive it back. Especially if the receiver is honorable, and who is more honorable than the LORD?

God is Keeping an Account!

God is aware when we don't use the gold and silver He has given to us. Remember that not everything that has been given to you is for your own use. It may be for another member of the Body of Christ. By holding it back you could be hurting yourself.

> *"Your gold and silver is _____; and the rust of them shall be a witness against you, and shall eat your flesh as it were fire. Ye have heaped treasure together for the last days."*
> **(James 5:3 KJV)**

If you don't use your money for tithes and offerings, God will be aware of it.

> *8 "Will a man rob God? Yet ye have robbed me. But ye say, Wherein have we robbed thee? In tithes and offerings.*
> *9 **Ye are cursed with a curse**: for ye have robbed me, even this whole nation.*
> *10 Bring ye all the tithes into the storehouse, that there may be meat in mine house, and prove me now herewith, saith the Lord of hosts, if I will not open you the windows of heaven, and pour you out a blessing, that there shall not be room enough to receive it.*
> *11 And I will rebuke the devourer for your sakes, and he shall not destroy the fruits of your ground; neither shall your vine cast her fruit before the time in the field, saith the Lord of hosts.*
> *12 And all nations shall call you blessed: for ye shall be a delightsome land, saith the Lord of hosts."*
> **(Malachi 3:8-12 KJV)**

14. How do we "rob" God? _____

_____

15. What happens to us when we rob God? _____

_____

16. Why do we bring the tithes into the storehouse? _____
_____

17. What does God promise that He will do for us when we bring in all the tithes and offerings into His house? _____
_____

> "For God gives wisdom and knowledge and joy to a man who is good in His sight; but to the sinner He gives the work of gathering and collecting, that he may give to him who is good before God. This also is vanity and grasping for the wind."
> **(Ecclesiastes 2:26 NKJV)**

As we work for God and disperse His wealth, we can also enjoy the benefits of that prosperity.

> 18 "Here is what I have seen: It is good and fitting for one to eat and drink, and to enjoy the good of all his labor in which he toils under the sun all the days of his life which God gives him; for it is his heritage.1
> 19 As for every man to whom God has given riches and wealth, and given him power to eat of it, to receive his heritage and rejoice in his labor — this is the gift of God."
> **(Ecclesiastes 5:18-19 NKJV)**

Reflections
1. Where does it say in scripture that we have an account?
2. Why could Paul say that fruit was being put into the Philippians' account?
3. When we give, what type of interest do we receive in our accounts? (Luke 6:38 KJV)
4. If we sow sparingly, how shall we receive?
5. When we sow abundantly, how shall we receive?

Applications
Ask the Lord if there is anything that He would like you to put into your bank account in heaven.
Ask what you should give and to whom.
Remember to be cheerful as this will bless your life and those that you help.

Memory Verse

"Give, and it shall be given unto you; good measure, pressed down, and shaken together, and running over, shall men give into your bosom. For with the same measure that ye mete withal it shall be measured to you again".
(Luke 6:38 KJV)

Closing Prayer

Dear Father, I don't want to be like the rich young man, who was not able to give. I don't want my gold, silver and money to be a witness against me. Help me to give freely to the causes that are dear to your heart. Lead me by your Holy Spirit to support the works of Your Kingdom. Help me to be a cheerful giver. I ask that in the name of Jesus. Amen.

How Do We Obtain Prosperity?
Chapter Six – Study Guide

Opening Prayer

　　Dear Father, help me to study your word and learn how to prosper. I desire to be approved of You, a worker who needs not to be ashamed. I ask for this in the name of Jesus. Amen.

The following questions will be answered during study of this chapter:
1. How often should we read the Holy Bible?
2. Who is going to make you prosperous?
3. How will you have good success?
4. Who should we give our tithes and offerings to?
5. Who else should we give to?

Study the Word

God has put His wisdom into the Holy Bible. Therefore, it's important to know what the Holy Bible has to say about obtaining prosperity.

> 7 *"Only be thou strong and very courageous*, **that thou mayest**
>
> _____ _____ _____ ____ ____
> _____ _____*, which Moses my servant commanded thee: turn not from it to the right hand or to the left, that thou mayest prosper whithersoever thou goest.*
> *8 This book of the law shall not depart out of thy mouth; but thou shalt meditate therein day and night,* **that thou mayest observe to do** *according to all that is written therein: for then* _____
> _____ _____ _____ _____ **prosperous,** *and then thou shalt have good success."*
> **(Joshua 1:7-8 KJV)**

1. How often should we meditate in the book of the law? _____
_____ _____

2. Why should we do that? That thou _____ _____ ____
_____ _____ _____ _____ _____ _____
_____ _____.

3. If we observe to do according to all that is written therein, what will happen to us? _____

_____

4. Who exactly is going to make us prosperous? _____

God instructed Joshua to be strong and very courageous, that he would observe to do according to all the Law, which Moses commanded.

It is important for us to be strong and very courageous. The Holy Bible will often tell us to do something that requires courage from us. For example, are we willing to tithe when our finances are looking bleak? Or do we lean on our own understanding instead? God is looking for a people who will obey His Word without moving to the right hand or to the left. Can we accept the fact that He always knows what's best? If we observe to do according to all that is in the Holy Bible, then we will prosper wherever we go. But as James said, we must be doers of the Word and not just listeners. It is the application of the Word that will help, not just the reading of it.

So that Joshua could make sure he understood the Law in order to obey it, he was instructed not to let the Law depart out of his mouth and he was commanded to meditate upon it day and night.

Now let us look at *Psalm One*. Here is another passage that gives clear instructions to meditate in God's law both day and night.

> *1 **Blessed** is the man who walks not in the counsel of the ungodly, nor stands in the path of sinners, nor sits in the seat of the scornful;*
> *2 But his delight is in the law of the Lord, **and in His law he meditates day and night.***
> *3 He shall be like a tree planted by the rivers of water, that brings forth its fruit in its season, whose leaf also shall not wither; and **whatever he does shall prosper.***
> ***(Psalm 1:1-3 NKJV)***

5. What happens to the man who walks not in the counsel of the ungodly?

_____

The reading of God's Word should be like book ends holding the hours of each day. We should give our attention to it the first thing in the morning and the last thing at night.

To read the Holy Bible through once each year requires you to read only eighty-five verses a day. These verses can be read in as little as twenty to forty minutes. Reading the Holy Bible once a year should be an absolute minimum for anyone who wants to live a life of godliness and be able to teach His Word.

There are many things God wants to teach His people, but:

> *"11...we have much to say, and hard to explain, **since you have become dull of hearing.***
> *12 For though by this time you ought to be teachers, you need someone to teach you again the first principles of the oracles of God; and you have come to need milk and not solid food."*
> *(Hebrews 5:11-12 NKJV)*

We can read here the frustration of the writer of *Hebrews* (i.e. God).

You have become dull of hearing....You ought to be teachers. God wants to teach us more, yet we haven't learnt the first principles properly. One can't teach algebra to the child who has forgotten how to add and subtract.

> *"_____ to shew thyself _____ unto God, a workman that needeth not to be ashamed, rightly dividing the word of truth."*
> *(2 Timothy 2:15 KJV)*

6. What does the workman need to do in order not to be ashamed?

_____

7. When we study, what word does God used to commend us?

_____

Finally God told Joshua to

> *"...observe to do according to all that is written therein: for **then thou shalt** make thy way prosperous, and then thou shalt have good success."*
> *(Joshua 1:8 KJV)*

When we observe to do according to all that is written in the Word, when we scrutinize and inspect our lives to see that we are doing all that is written in the Holy Bible, then *we* make our way prosperous, and *we* will have good success.

God does *not* promise to make us prosperous. Notice that it is *ourselves* that make our way prosperous! When we *do* the things that are commanded to us in the Holy Bible! I cannot overemphasize the fact that it is not God who prospers us; it is ourselves who prosper ourselves, *if* we obey what God commands us to do in the Holy Bible.

Seeking the Lord

> *3 "Sixteen years old was Uzziah when he began to reign, and he reigned fifty and two years in Jerusalem...*
> *4 And he did that which was right in the sight of the Lord,...*
> *5 And he sought God in the days of Zechariah, ...: and as long as he sought the Lord, God made him to prosper."*
> *(2 Chronicles 26:3-5 KJV)*

This is something we see over and over again in the Old Testament. The kings of Israel and Judah who chose to seek God always prospered. On the other hand, those who did evil and did not seek the LORD, would see a decline. *(See the chapter on Kings.)*

Consider the problems Joshua had at the city of Ai and with the Gibeonites. Both of these problems would have been avoided if he had sought the Lord *before* the events. *(See Joshua 7, 8, and 9.)*

8. Which King was always inquiring of the Lord? Always seeking Him, inquiring and seeking saving himself a great deal of trouble. *(See 1 Samuel 23:1-13.)* _____

Giving

If you want to prosper as a Christian, you must have a soul that gives willingly. We need to be rich towards God, rich towards the poor, and rich in every good work.

I have heard people say that they only want enough to meet their own needs. Can you see how outrageously selfish this is? Only enough for themselves!

Who is going to provide money for the Church, for the poor, for every good work God wants to do through us?

We know from *Joshua 1:7-8* that we need to observe to do according to all that is written in the Law. But what does the Bible say about prospering?

> *"_____, and it shall be _____ unto you; good measure, pressed down, and shaken together, and running over, shall men give into your bosom. For with the same measure that ye mete withal it shall be measured to you again."*
> *(Luke 6:38 KJV)*

So here again we see the wonders of the wisdom of God. He has decided to prosper His children when they give! What an incredible law.

Every caring father wants to increase the prosperity of his children and wants them to be generous, which would be their safeguard against greed. In the same way God has set a law that prospers His children as they give.

Isn't that amazing, especially when you consider the fact that giving and greed are opposites.

> "Beloved, I wish _____ _____ _____ that thou
> mayest prosper and be in health, even as thy soul prospereth."
> **(3 John 1:2 KJV)**

As our soul prospers, as we learn to give, God prospers us in direct proportion to our giving.

The same measure we use is measured to us.

Have you ever noticed the structure of *Luke 6:38*? On the one side we have "give" and on the other "given to you," "good measure," "pressed down," "shaken together," "running over," and "shall men give into your bosom."

This is somewhat similar to a farmer sowing seed. You don't receive just one seed back for each seed sown. Sometimes it is thirty-fold, sixty-fold even one hundred-fold!

God loves to give. Jesus told us that unless a grain of wheat falls into the ground and dies, it remains alone, but if it dies, it bears much fruit. *(See John 12:24.)*

> "For God so loved the world, that he gave his only begotten Son, that
> whosoever believeth in him should not perish, but have everlasting life."
> **(John 3:16 KJV)**

Who should we give to?

We should give our tithes* and offerings* to the church we attend.* *(See the chapter on tithes and offerings.)*

We should give to the poor and needy.

We should give to good works such as Christian television, radio, evangelism, missionary work, hospitals, secular charities, the blind, etc.

God Gives

Sometimes you hear people say, "O God, if you give me a million dollars I will build you a hospital," or something similar.

What I would say to them in response is: "What are you doing with your

$10 or your $100?" If you are not giving with the little you have, you will never give when you have much more.

> *"One who is _____ in a very little is also _____*
> *in much, and one who is dishonest in a very little is also dishonest in*
> *much."*
> *(Luke 16:10 ESV)*

The widow who put her two mites into the treasury gave more than the rich people, because she gave according to what she had—she gave everything!

If you want to grow in prosperity, then grow in giving.

Do we believe what we preach and what we hear?

When I was a fairly new convert and a student, my pastor told me that I did not need to tithe, as I did not have very much money. My response even back then was, "Don't you want me to prosper?"

We can't preach that we prosper through giving and then tell the poor not to give! As a Church, we should encourage the poor to give, while not forgetting our obligation to them at the same time.

Let us see how God provided for Elijah (and the widow):

> *8 "Then the word of the Lord came to him, saying,*
> *9 Arise, go to Zarephath, which belongs to Sidon, and dwell there. See, I*
> *have commanded _____ _____ there to provide for you.*
> *10 So he arose and went to Zarephath. And when he came to the gate of*
> *the city, indeed a widow was there gathering sticks. And he called to her*
> *and said, "Please bring me a little water in a cup, that I may drink."*
> *11 And as she was going to get it, he called to her and said, "Please*
> *bring me a morsel of bread in your hand."*
> *12 So she said, "As the Lord your God lives, I do not have bread, only a*
> *handful of flour in a bin, and a little oil in a jar; and see, I am gathering*
> *a couple of sticks that I may go in and prepare it for myself and my son,*
> *that we may eat it, and die."*
> *13 And Elijah said to her, **"Do not fear;** go and do as you have said, but*
> ***make me a small cake from it first, and bring it to me;** and **afterward***
> *make some for yourself and your son.*
> *14 For thus says the Lord God of Israel: 'The bin of flour shall not be*
> *used up, nor shall the jar of oil run dry, until the day the Lord sends rain*
> *on the earth.'"*
> *15 So she went away and did according to the word of Elijah; and she*
> *and he and her household ate for many days. 16 The bin of flour was not*
> *used up, nor did the jar of oil run dry, according to the word of the Lord*
> *which He spoke by Elijah."*
> *(1 Kings 17:8-16 NKJV)*

9. What did the widow have to do *first* in order for God to then provide the miracle of provision for her and her household? _____

_____

It is better to teach and preach giving and prosperity than to foster a climate of dependency, notwithstanding our financial obligations.

Jesus became poor so that we could become rich. This was not just for those who have plenty to give, but for us all—from the poorest to the richest, without partiality.

Remember, He loves us all.

The Wisdom of Solomon

What does Solomon have to say about giving?

> 1 "_____ _____ _____ *upon the waters,*
> *For you will find it after many days.*
> 2 _____ _____ _____ _____ _____,
> *and also to eight,*
> *For you do not know what evil will be on the earth.*
> *3 If the clouds are full of rain,*
> *They empty themselves upon the earth;*
> *And if a tree falls to the south or the north,*
> *In the place where the tree falls, there it shall lie.*
> *4 He who observes the wind will not sow,*
> *And he who regards the clouds will not reap.*
> *5 As you do not know what is the way of the wind,*
> *Or how the bones grow in the womb of her who is with child,*
> *So you do not know the works of God who makes everything.*
> **6 In the morning** _____ _____ _____.
> **And in the evening do not withhold your hand;**
> *For you do not know which will prosper,*
> *Either this or that,*
> *Or whether both alike will be good. "*
> **(Ecclesiastes 11:1-6 NKJV)**

1. Cast your bread upon the waters, for you will find it after many days.

Is Solomon really talking about finding soggy bread? No, he means that we need to cast away from ourselves. Give, and you will get it back after a period of time. This is a confirmation of Luke 6:38, and this is a bit like feeding ducks. Throw your bread out, and in this way you will be feeding others. Don't worry; you will receive a reward after a period of time passes.

2. Give a serving to seven and also to eight, for you do not know what evil will be on the Earth.

Again, we are admonished to GIVE. This may mean that we should invite more people over for meals, especially those who cannot repay you. Develop a strategy that will lead to increase. Give to seven, to eight, then nine and ten. You do not know what will happen at any given time; you may suddenly be called to Heaven, or you may suddenly lose all your money. But if you have a good account* in Heaven, you will be all right. (See the chapter on your bank account.)

3. If the clouds are full of rain, they empty themselves upon the Earth; and if a tree falls to the south or the north, in the place where the tree falls, there it shall lie.

Where are the clouds? They are in the heavens where the birds fly. When Jesus said to the rich young man to give his money away to the poor, and that he would then have treasure in Heaven, *He did not say that he could not receive withdrawals* from his heavenly bank account!!

When your heavenly bank accounts (clouds) are full of giving (rain), they empty themselves upon the Earth. This is a law—a spiritual law. To confirm this law to us, we are told that if a tree falls to the south or the north, in the place where the tree falls, there it shall lie. What is Solomon talking about? He is talking about forces. What causes the tree to fall and remain where it falls? It is a great force, one of the principles of physics—the law of gravity.

To confirm to us the spiritual law of giving and receiving back to Earth, God has chosen to compare it with the *universal* law of gravity. It is always in force, and it never changes.

Think about it.

More Verses on How to Prosper

"Pray _____ _____ _____ ____ _____: they shall prosper that love thee."
(Psalm 122:6 KJV)

"In the _____ sow thy seed, and in the evening withhold not thine hand: for thou knowest not whether shall prosper, either this or that, or whether they both shall be alike good."
(Ecclesiastes 11:6 KJV)

10. When should we sow our seed? _____

Do not wait to work, do it straight away. Do not wait until you are in financial trouble, give straight away. Build your life on the rock of the scriptures.

> 18 *"Riches and honour are with me; yea, durable riches and righteousness.*
> 19 *My fruit is better than gold, yea, than fine gold; and my revenue than choice silver.*
> 20 *I lead in the way of righteousness, in the midst of the paths of judgment:*
> 21 *That I may cause those that love me to inherit substance; and I will fill their treasures."*
> **(Proverbs 8:18-21 KJV)**

11. Who is God talking about in *Proverbs 8:18-21*? _____

_____

Solomon also confirms what we learned from the patriarchs that hard work is sometimes needed.

> *"He becometh poor that dealeth with a _____ _____: but the hand of the diligent maketh rich."*
> **(Proverbs 10:4 KJV)**

Laziness does not prosper us.

> *"By _____ and _____ _____ of the Lord are riches, and honour, and life."*
> **(Proverbs 22:4 KJV)**

> 19 *"Lay not up for yourselves treasures _____ _____, where moth and rust doth corrupt, and where thieves break through and steal:*
> 20 *But lay up for yourselves treasures in heaven, where neither moth nor rust doth corrupt, and where thieves do not break through nor steal:*
> 21 ***For where your treasure is, there will your heart be also."***
> **(Matthew 6:19-21 KJV)**

> *"Not because I desire a gift: but ___ _____ fruit that may abound to your account."*
> **(Philippians 4:17 KJV)**

12. Who is it that desires fruit in your account? _____

As the scriptures are written by men 'moved by God', then who ultimately wants fruit in your account? _____

As you give freely to others God will give freely to you.

" But my God shall supply all your need according to his riches in glory by Christ Jesus."
(Philippians 4:19 KJV)

13. Who is it that desires fruit in your account? _____

As the scriptures are written by men 'moved by God', then who ultimately wants fruit in your account? _____

As you give freely to others God will give freely to you.

" But my God shall supply all your need according to his riches in glory by Christ Jesus."
(Philippians 4:19 KJV)

How Do We Keep Our Prosperity?

"... Thus saith God, Why _____ ___ _____ _____ of the Lord, that ye cannot prosper? because ye have forsaken the Lord, he hath also forsaken you."
(2 Chronicles 24:20 KJV)

14. Why could they not prosper?
_____

*" He that _____ his sins **shall not prosper**: but whoso confesseth and forsaketh them shall have mercy."*
(Proverbs 28:13 KJV)

15. What should we NOT do with our sins? _____

16. What should we do with our sins? _____

17. In summary, how do we obtain prosperity? Fill in your understanding from the following verses:

Verse One:
7 "Only be thou strong and very courageous, that thou mayest observe to do according to all the law, which Moses my servant commanded thee: turn not from it to the right hand or to the left, that thou mayest prosper whithersoever thou goest.
8 This book of the law shall not depart out of thy mouth; but thou shalt meditate therein day and night, that thou mayest observe to do according

to all that is written therein: for then thou shalt make thy way prosperous, and then thou shalt have good success."
(Joshua 1:7-8 KJV)

_____

_____

Verse Two:

"And he sought God in the days of Zechariah, who had understanding in the visions of God: and as long as he sought the Lord, God made him to prosper."
(2 Chronicles 26:5 KJV)

_____

_____

Verse Three:

"Give, and it shall be given unto you; good measure, pressed down, and shaken together, and running over, shall men give into your bosom. For with the same measure that ye mete withal it shall be measured to you again."
(Luke 6:38 KJV

_____

_____

Verse Four:

18 "Riches and honour are with me; yea, durable riches and righteousness.
19 My fruit is better than gold, yea, than fine gold; and my revenue than choice silver.
20 I lead in the way of righteousness, in the midst of the paths of judgment:
21 That I may cause those that love me to inherit substance; and I will fill their treasures."
(Proverbs 8:18-21 KJV)

_____

_____

Verse Five:

By humility and the fear of the Lord are riches, and honour, and life.
(Proverbs 22:4 KJV)

_____

_____

Verse Six:

> *Pray for the peace of Jerusalem: they shall prosper that love thee.*
> **(Psalm 122:6 KJV)**

_____

_____

Verse Seven:

> *19 Lay not up for yourselves treasures upon earth, where moth and rust doth corrupt, and where thieves break through and steal:*
> *20 But lay up for yourselves treasures in heaven, where neither moth nor rust doth corrupt, and where thieves do not break through nor steal:*
> *21 For where your treasure is, there will your heart be also.*
> **(Matthew 6:19-21 KJV)**

_____

_____

17. In review, what are the keys to prosperity given to the patriarchs?

Noah   _____

Abraham   _____

Isaac   _____

Jacob   _____

Joseph   _____

Reflections

1. How often should we read the Holy Bible?
2. Who is going to make you prosperous?
3. How will you have good success?
4. Who should we give our tithes and offerings to?
5. Who else should we give to?

Applications

Be disciplined in reading the word, and especially obeying the word. Plan to invite people for dinner, especially the more unfortunate who cannot reciprocate.

Make sure that the Lord's Prayer is part of your daily time with the Lord. Ask for forgiveness and for the grace you need to forgive others *(See Matthew 6:9-14 KJV)*.

Memory Verses

7 "Only be thou strong and very courageous, that thou mayest observe to do according to all the law, which Moses my servant commanded thee: whithersoever thou goest.

8 This book of the law shall not depart out of thy mouth; but thou shalt meditate therein day and night, that thou mayest observe to do according to all that is written therein: for then thou shalt make thy way prosperous, and then thou shalt have good success."

(Joshua 1:7-8 KJV)

Closing Prayer

Dear Father, you say in your word to ask. I ask you Father, help me to be obedient to your word that I may prosper. Help me to be wise and give to the poor. Show me by your Holy Spirit what to do. I ask for these things in the name of Jesus. Amen

Tithes, Offerings, and Firstfruits
Giving to God
Chapter Seven – Study Guide

Opening Prayer

  Dear Father, Your Word is perfect and a delight to my soul. Open my eyes to see the wisdom you have put in tithes and offerings. Relationships are about giving and receiving. Help me to understand how I can give into Your Kingdom. I ask this in the name of Jesus. Amen.

The following questions will be answered during study of this chapter:
1. What is a tithe?
2. Who does the tithe belong to?
3. What is the tithe for?
4. What do the ministers and musicians do when the tithe does not come in?
5. Under which priesthood was the tithe revealed?
6. Which priesthood is Jesus the High Priest of?
7. If we want to get God's attention, what can we do?
8. What is an example of an atoning offering?
9. What is an example of a relational offering?

Tithing

In the beginning of Genesis we can see in the account of Cain and Abel that what differentiates one man from another is often their attitudes regarding giving to God.

As a Christian, how easy is it to want to receive from God. We pray, "Forgive me, heal *me*, bless ME, etc. . . ." But where are those who love to give to God?

The Wise Men brought gold, frankincense, and myrrh to Jesus. The things we can give God are gold (our money), frankincense (living a consecrated life), and myrrh (our willingness to suffer on His behalf).

One way we can give God our money is through tithes. A tithe literally means, a tenth of all income we receive in any way.

1. The first mention of this word in the Bible occurs when Abraham gives a tithe after his battle in *Genesis 14*:

> *18 Then Melchizedek king of Salem brought out bread and wine; he was the priest of God Most High.*
> *19 And he blessed him and said:"Blessed be Abram of God Most High, Possessor of heaven and earth;*
> *20 And blessed be God Most High, Who has delivered your enemies into your hand." And _____ _____ _____ _____ ___*
> *_____ _____."*
> **(Genesis 14:18-20 NKJV)**

2. What three things did Melchizedek give to Abraham? _____

_____   _____

3. What did Abraham give to Melchizedek?_____

_____

4. Abram *(before God changed his name to Abraham)* gave a tithe of all that he won in the battle with the Kings. He gave it to the priest of God, Melchizedek, who in turn blessed him and ministered the bread and the wine to him. Sound familiar?

> *4 "And no man taketh this honour unto himself, but he that is called of God, as was Aaron.*
> *5 So also Christ glorified not himself to be made an high priest; but he that said unto him, Thou art my Son, to day have I begotten thee.*
> *6 As he saith also in another place, Thou art a priest for ever_____*
> *_____ _____ ____ _____."*
> **(Hebrews 5:4-6 KJV)**

5. After which order is Jesus the high priest? _____

> *20 "And Jacob vowed a vow, saying, If God will be with me, and will keep me in this way that I go, and will give me bread to eat, and raiment to put on,*
> *21 So that I come again to my father's house in peace; then shall the Lord be my God:*
> *22 And this stone, which I have set for a pillar, shall be God's house:*
> **and of all that thou shalt give me I will _____ give _____**
> **_____ unto thee."**
> **(Genesis 28:20-22 KJV)**

6. What did Jacob promise to give God for blessing him? _____

_____

_____

7. Next, we see God setting up tithing in the Law through Moses:

> *30 "And _____ _____ _____ of the land, whether of the seed*
> *of the land or of the fruit of the tree, _____ _____ _____ . It*
> *is holy to the Lord.*
> *31 If a man wants at all to redeem any of his tithes, he shall add one-fifth*
> *to it.*
> *32 And concerning the tithe of the herd or the flock, of whatever passes*
> *under the rod, **the tenth one** shall be holy to the Lord."*
> ***(Leviticus 27:30-32 NKJV)***

8. Who does the tithe belong to? _____

9. What special word is used to describe the tithe? _____

In our modern times, the fruit of our labor is more conventionally paid to us through our wages. Though we must remember not only to give to God what we have earned, but also whatever comes from other means, gifts, dividends, finding something, etc.—any and all income.

God finds many different ways to bless us, and we should be grateful to Him for each of these things in our tithes.

When I was a student, my pastor told me that because I only had a little money I should not tithe out of my grant. I was quite affronted by this, as I had believed his teaching that you prosper as you give. I wondered, "Does he not want me to prosper?!" (Remember the poor widow.)

In spite of what he said to me, I continued tithing, and in approximately my first year of tithing I earned $7,000.

In my second year of tithing I earned $5,000.

In my third year of tithing on a single day I earned approximately $200,000!

It is impossible to out-give our God. But what is the purpose of bringing the tithe to church?

"Behold, I have given the children of Levi all the tithes in Israel as an **inheritance** _____   _____   _____ _____ _____

_____ _____ _____ , *the work of the tabernacle of*

meeting."
(Numbers 18:21 NKJV)

10. Why were the tithes given to the children of Levi? _____

_____

_____

"...for the Levites should receive the tithes...For the children of Israel and the children of Levi shall bring the offering of the grain, of the new wine and the oil, to the storerooms where the articles of the sanctuary are, **where the priests who minister and the gatekeepers and the singers are; and** _____ _____ _____ _____ _____

_____ _____ _____ _____ ."

(Nehemiah 10:39 NKJV)

11. In addition to the priests, who else received from the tithes?

_____

_____

12. When we don't give our tithes what happens to the house of God?

_____

_____

10 "I also realized that the portions for the Levites had not been given them; for **each of the Levites and the singers who did the work had**

_____ _____ _____ _____ _____ .

11 So I contended with the rulers, and said, **"Why is the house of God forsaken?"** *"*
(Nehemiah 13:10-11a NKJV)

13. What do the ministers and musicians do when the tithe is not brought in? _____

_____

The tithes are for those who work in the house of God—the ministers, the doorkeepers, and the musicians—all who minister the Gospel of Jesus Christ. As God said through Paul and Moses:

9 "For it is written in the law of Moses, "You shall not muzzle an ox while it treads out the grain." Is it oxen God is concerned about?

10 Or does He say it altogether for our sakes? For our sakes, no doubt, this is written, that he who plows should plow in hope, and he who threshes in hope should be partaker of his hope.
11 If we have sown spiritual things for you, is it a great thing if we _____ _____ _____ _____ *."*
   (1 Corinthians 9:9-11 NKJV)

When we don't bring the tithe into the church, then something has to give, and that normally means that the leaders and musicians who should be laboring in word and prayers have to go and work in the secular environment to provide for their households.

We all lose out! We need our leaders to be in the Word and in prayer—on their knees as often as possible.

Another way of looking at it is to think about who owns the tithe.

14. Who does the tithe belong to? _____ The Bible gives us clear answers to this question:

   "And all the tithe of the land, whether of the seed of the land or of the fruit of the tree, ____ _____ _____ . It is holy to the Lord."
   (Leviticus 27:30 NKJV)

I particularly like the New International Version translation here:

   "'A tithe of everything from the land, whether grain from the soil or fruit from the trees, _____ to the Lord; it is holy to the Lord. "
   (Leviticus 27:30 NIV)

We see here that the Bible says that the tithe belongs to the Lord: it is His, not ours! It is not ours to give, but it is for us to return it to Him.

When we don't return what does not belong to us, we are involved in stealing. Does that seem like a strong thing for me to say? Let's look in the Book of Malachi to get our answer:

   "Will a man _____ God?
   Yet you have robbed Me! But you say,
   'In what way have we robbed You?' In _____ and
   _____ ."
   (Malachi 3:8 NKJV)

Very simply, this means: One for God, nine for me. One for God, nine for me. One for God, nine for me. One for God, nine for me. One for God, nine for me. One for God, nine for me. One for God, nine for me.

Not such a bad deal, really.

There are some who would suggest that we don't have to tithe, because tithing is part of the Law.

Well, yes. Tithing is part of the Law, as are not committing adultery, loving God, and honoring your mother and father.

As we have already seen, tithing was here on the Earth before the Law came into being. In fact, tithing was revealed to us in the same breath as the Melchizedek priesthood was revealed to us. This priesthood, which ministered the bread and the wine and received tithes, is the same priesthood that is now in existence. In fact, the only commandment we know about this priesthood is that they should receive tithes!!!

Jesus is the High Priest of the Melchizedek priesthood. *(See Hebrews 6-7.)*

In our lives we learn to turn our life into money through our work. We exchange our time—a portion of our life—into money.

It seems right that as Abram received the bread and the wine, representing Jesus' life, that Abram should also give the tithes, representing his life.

As Jesus has given us his life, his flesh and blood, it is only right that we should give him our life, money earned throughout time (life).

As a businessman, I would say this seems to be a good contract.

Offerings

Now that we have looked at tithing, what other types of offerings does the Bible discuss?

As we study the Law of Moses, we see that there were many kinds of offerings. How do these offerings affect us now, in the New Covenant?

> Atonement Money,
> Burnt Offerings,
> Drink Offering,
> Free Offerings,
> Freewill Offerings,
> Heave Offering,
> Meat Offering,
> Grain Offering,
> Offer Praise,
> Offer Sacrifices of Joy,
> Offer Sacrifices of Righteousness,
> Offer Unto God Thanksgivings,
> Offer Up Spiritual Sacrifices,
> Offered Incense,

Offered Themselves,
Offering Made by Fire,
Offering of Jealousy,
Offering of Memorial,
Passover Offerings,
Peace Offerings,
Sacrifice of Thanksgiving,
Sin/Trespass Offering,
Thank Offerings,
The First of Thy Ripe Fruits, Liquors and Firstborn,
Voluntary Offerings,
Vows,
Wave Offering,
Wood Offering.

In looking at the offerings that have been given to God from the beginning of time, we can see that many of them are no longer relevant because of Jesus' sacrifice as the Lamb of God. Therefore, there is no more offering for sin.

For me, the most appropriate way to categorize them is: 1) atoning positional offerings, and 2) relational offerings.

Examples of Atoning Offerings

Sin/Trespass Offerings. These are no longer relevant because Jesus' blood redeems us.

> *"Sacrifice and offering and burnt offerings and offering for sin thou wouldest not, neither hadst pleasure therein; which are offered by the law; ...We are sanctified through the offering of the body of Jesus Christ once for all.... But this man, after he had offered one sacrifice for sins for ever, sat down on the right hand of God; ... Now where remission of these is, there is ___ _____ _____ _____ _____."*
> *(Hebrews 10:5-18 KJV)*

The burnt offering (Hebrew עֹלָה - *olah*) involves the whole animal being burnt.

The drink offering—this involves wine usually presented with a burnt offering.

Wave and Heave offerings were particular parts of the offerings that were either waved or heaved (lifted up and down) to the Lord. These parts, the breast and the shoulder, were eaten by the priests and their families.

Examples of Relational Offerings

Free-will Offerings—this type of offering, as the name suggests, is one that comes from a person's free will. An example of this is seen when Moses collected gold, silver, brass, and precious stones for the work of building the Tabernacle in the wilderness. *(See Exodus 35)*.

In this type of offering, nobody was compelled to bring anything; it was for those with willing hearts—those who want to give to God. This is a quite common type of offering for those of us in the New Testament in cases where money is raised for a good work or project. For example, in the church I attend, we regularly give an offering to help the poor who are living on the streets of London.

Vows

A vow is a promise we make to God. Usually it follows this format: IF you do this, I WILL do that.

Jacob promised to give God a tenth of his income if God would bless him.

Hannah promised that if God gave her a son, she would give the child to Him.

Jephthah promised that if God would give him victory over Ammon, then he would offer as a burnt offering "whatsoever comes out of the doors of his house."(This turned out to be his daughter!)

A Note of Warning

One day I was boasting to a friend about God's ability to do anything. When I said that "God could give to me a pair of Prestige clarinets within a day, and that when he would do so, I would ring her to let her know." I said this so that she would see the power of God. Bear in mind that I was a student with no financial means of my own and that these clarinets cost approximately $10,000.00!

Within the same day my agent rang me to say that the company who manufactured these clarinets would sponsor me by giving them to me. I was very pleased, but I forgot to tell my friend!

For various reasons I did not receive those clarinets after all! A couple of years later I was again offered these clarinets and again it did not happen. After the third attempt failed, I was talking to God about it saying how strange it was that every time I tried to get these clarinets something went wrong, when he reminded me of my vow that I would ring my friend when God first came through! As I remembered my mistake I inwardly blushed. I had made a promise to God and broken it.

4 "When you make a vow to God, do not delay to pay it; For He has no pleasure in fools. Pay what you have vowed.
5 Better _____ _____ _____ than to vow and not pay."
(Ecclesiastes 5:4-5 NKJV)

After praying and repenting of my sin, I received the new clarinets very quickly!

You see, not paying my vow caused a blockage in my life. When I repented, the blockage was removed.

What is it that moves us to bring offerings to God?

Offerings are made to God in Genesis before the Law, according to the Law of Moses and in the New Testament, as well.

What Are Offerings For? Do We Give Offerings Now?

The Law is really quite simple to follow: do this, do that, then do the next thing. But how did Abel and Cain know about giving offerings to God? The truth is we don't know how they knew. There is no account of them learning it from their parents, Adam and Eve, yet "In the process of time they brought an offering." Either they learned it from their parents, or they learned it directly from God, or it was already stored in their souls in the same way that birds know when to fly south and where to go.

Why did they give to God? Surely God doesn't need anything? Do their offerings involve created beings helping out the Creator a bit? I don't think so, yet we are given the opportunity to give to Him, which is a marvelous privilege indeed.

We see from the account of Abel and Cain, that when Abel had given his offering to God, the Lord had respect for Abel and his offering. On the other hand, when Cain brought his offering, he and his offering **were not** respected.

> *2 "Then she bore again, this time his brother Abel. Now Abel was a keeper of sheep, but Cain was a tiller of the ground.*
> *3 And in the process of time it came to pass that Cain brought an offering of the fruit of the ground to the Lord.*
> *4 Abel also brought of the firstborn of his flock _____ _____ _____*
> *_____ . And the Lord respected Abel and his offering,*
> *5 but He did not respect Cain and his offering. And Cain was very angry, and his countenance fell.*
> *6 So the Lord said to Cain, "Why are you angry? And why has your countenance fallen?*
> *7 If you do well, will you not be accepted? And if you do not do well, sin lies at the door. And its desire is for you, but you should rule over it."*
> **(Genesis 4:2-7 NKJV)**

15. What do we know about the quality of the flock that Abel brought?

_____

Where Do You Belong?

With maturity comes responsibility. In any group, whether it's a family, a nation, or a kingdom, there is a responsibility to make a contribution to the general upkeep. In a family we share the bills, in a nation we pay our taxes, and in a kingdom we show our allegiance by our support.

Abel did not just bring his contribution; he carefully chose the best, the fattest. He and his offering were respected. Though most of the Kingdom of Heaven was situated in the stars above, his commitment to God and God's kingdom was shown through the quality of his contribution.

Exactly what was wrong with Cain's offering we are not sure. Suffice to say that the Lord did not respect his contribution and in turn he was not respected or accepted. Though not accepted, Cain was not rejected. "If you do well, will you not be accepted?" The alternative to not being accepted in God's society is to be a member of the other community. "If you do not do well, sin lies at the door. And its desire is for you, but you should rule over it."

Note here how sin is personified: "Its desire is for you." Make no mistake about it: sin wants you. It wants to own you. Remember the Scripture that tells us that when we sin, we become a slave to the sin. *(See John 8:34.)*

God does not need our money, *but*, by giving us the opportunity to give to Him, He is in fact honoring us by giving us the room to be contributors. We are citizens and we become shareholders in the Kingdom of God!

If we hold back and are selfish, then we are not deemed **accepted**?! Where is our allegiance?

The first recorded thing that Noah did after coming out of the ark was to offer burnt offerings of every clean animal and bird to the LORD.

In a burnt offering the animal is completely burnt up; nothing is left—just ashes. Through this means it was thought that the animal was being offered up completely to God. Does this mean that the spirit of the animal went to be with God in Heaven? Having not been to Heaven, it is difficult for anyone to confirm this. Solomon said,

> *"Who knows if the spirit of man rises upward and if the spirit of the animal goes down into the earth?"*
> *(Ecclesiastes 3:21 NIV)*

Who knows?

Well, God knows.

Whatever happens to the spirit of the animal when it is burnt is, of course, completely within God's control, for that animal has passed over to Him.

So why did Noah offer these animals to God? We know from Genesis 7 that Noah entered the ark with two of every unclean animal and seven of every clean animal. So why did he think he could spare one of every clean animal to be given over to God?

From *Genesis 7:11* and *Genesis 8:13-14*, we can see that Noah was in the ark for slightly over one year! What an experience that must have been. How many people do you suppose were on the Earth before the flood? We know that there were enough people to fill the earth with violence. *(See Genesis 6:11.)*

It is difficult to know whether that means there were more people alive then than now or less.

But to fill the Earth with anything would require a lot of people.

Imagine the thoughts of Noah while he was in the ark. Apart from the seven people, seven of each of the clean animals, and two of each of the unclean animals that were within the ark, every other person and animal drowned. Was it billions of people? It might well have been.

"Why was I saved—why me?" must have been a question that was in the minds of those on board the ark.

He has one year to contemplate the enormity of the situation. But remember, he did attempt to find out, by sending forth the birds, when the end of his confinement would take place. He did not know that it would only be one year! Like everyone who experiences prolonged confinement, I'm sure he must have been thinking, "What is the first thing I am going to do when I am released?"

The first recorded thing Noah did was to build an altar and offer as burnt offerings one of every clean animal.

It was a mixture of gratitude and the fear of the Lord.

Let us consider how God reacted to the offering. First of all, He was not happy with mankind.

> 5 *"And God saw that the wickedness of man was great in the earth, and that* _____ _____ *of the thoughts of his heart was* _____ _____ *continually.*
> 6 *And it repented the Lord that he had made man on the earth, and it grieved him at his heart.*

7 And the Lord said, I will destroy man whom I have created from the face of the earth; both man, and beast, and the creeping thing, and the fowls of the air; for it repenteth me that I have made them."
(Genesis 6:5-7 KJV)

We know from the Scriptures that God is very longsuffering. He is always ready to forgive, and He is full of mercy. At this point He must have been very fed up. He knew what was happening on the Earth: evil, violence, evil thoughts, and wickedness.

God had been putting up with man's evil thoughts for a long time. Even after the plan for the ark was put into operation, there were years waiting for the completion of the construction of the ark. During this time the Earth was full of evil.

When you create millions and billions of souls and they are continually evil, except for one man, it must be extremely disappointing. It truly grieved God in His heart. He also said that he repented of making mankind. At first the idea that God repented of making us is quite shocking. But I think this is explained in *Genesis 6:6* where He says that He repents of making us on the Earth. Perhaps he had considered making us in Heaven rather than on the Earth? I don't think we can imagine the burden and grief that God had to endure during this time. Even after the destruction of so many souls, we know that there was a period of just over a year before life returned to the Earth through the ark. We should consider what was happening in the Spirit realm during this time. It must have been quite some administration and processing feat to cope with so many souls passing over all at the same time. Remember, it took six days to create this world, but this was a period of just over a year!!

So in response to all of this, Noah offers up one of each of the clean animals as a burnt offering.

20 "And Noah builded an altar unto the Lord; and took of every clean beast, and of every clean fowl, and _____ _____ _____ on the altar.
21 And the Lord smelled a sweet savour; and the Lord said in his heart, I will not again curse the ground any more for man's sake; for the imagination of man's heart is evil from his youth; neither will I again smite any more every thing living, as I have done.
22 While the earth remaineth, seedtime and harvest, and cold and heat, and summer and winter, and day and night shall not cease.
And _____ _____ _____ and his sons, and said unto them, Be fruitful, and multiply, and replenish the earth."
(Genesis 8:20-22 KJV)

And the LORD smelled a sweet savour. What do you think God could smell? Was it burning meat? God could smell something pleasant from the Earth. That smell was a man doing something that was not evil, doing something that was not self-motivated. It was the sweet aroma of a man trying to give something back to Him! Well, that changes the whole picture.

God describes the sensation He receives when we give something to Him as being of a sweet-smelling savour. What smells pleasant to most of us? Perhaps a rose, perfume, incense? When we're hungry, the aroma of a good meal smells good. God immediately responds to this offering by saying:

> *"I will not again _____ _____ _____ any more for man's sake... And God _____ Noah and his sons, and said unto them, Be fruitful, and multiply, and replenish the earth."*
> **(Genesis 8:21-22 KJV)**

The next mention of offerings is one of the big tests of mankind. Would a man love and trust God enough to offer up "his only begotten son."
man to whom this test came was Abraham. As we know, he passed the test with flying colors because he was willing to offer up his only begotten son to God.

> *15 "Then the Angel of the Lord called to Abraham a second time out of heaven,*
> *16 and said:"By _____ ____ _____ _____ sworn, says the Lord, because you have done this thing, and have not withheld your son, your only son —*
> *17 _____ ____ _____ _____ _____, and multiplying I will multiply your descendants as the stars of the heaven and as the sand which is on the seashore; and your descendants shall possess the gate of their enemies.*
> *18 In your seed all the nations of the earth shall be blessed, because you have _____ My voice."*
> **(Genesis 22:15-18 NKJV)**

16. Who did God swear by? _____

On request we see Abraham offering up such a precious gift to God. But God's response, as in the case of Noah, was to bless the giver.

> *1"So Israel took his journey with all that he had, and came to Beersheba, and _____ _____ to the God of his father Isaac.*
> *2 Then God spoke to Israel in the visions of the night, and said, "Jacob, Jacob!" And he said, "Here I am."*
> *3 So He said, "I am God, the God of your father; do not fear to go down to Egypt, for I will make of you a great nation there.*
> *4 I will go down with you to Egypt, and I will also surely bring you up again; and Joseph will put his hand on your eyes."*
> **(Genesis 46:1-4 NKJV)**

17. Did God respond to Israel before or after Israel had made sacrifices to Him? _____

When we offer something to God, God responds to us. This is a very important precept. If you need a response from God then give Him an offering. You will get His attention, that you are serious.

Firstfruits

The first mention of firstfruits in the Bible is found in *Exodus 23*, when God asks Moses to set up three feasts in the year. It is the second of these feasts—"The feast of Harvest," in which the children of Israel were required to bring in the firstfruits from their labors in the field.

After the firstfruits of the harvest were collected, they were given to Aaron and to his descendants, the priests who minister in the house of God. They presented a small portion of the offering, a memorial, to God with the remainder to be eaten by them and their families.

From Nehemiah we can see that the ministers who received the firstfruits also included the gatekeepers and singers.

> 10 "I also realized that the portions for the Levites _____ _____ _____ _____ _____; for each of the Levites and the singers who did the work had gone back to his field.
> 11 So I contended with the rulers, and said, **"Why is the house of God forsaken?"**
> *(Nehemiah 13: 10-11a NKJV)*

When we neglect the house of God, those who are chosen to do the work have to find secular work to fulfil their needs!

Are the churches filled with choirs and orchestras, or do the musicians work in the world for their living and do part-time work for the churches? Is your pastor fully supported by the church, or does he have other part-time or full-time work to do to support himself and his family?

When you get a new job or start a new business venture, consider how to apportion the firstfruits unto the Lord.

> *Being grateful to God in this way*
> *pleases Him and helps support His Church.*

Reflections

1. What is a tithe?
2. Who does the tithe belong to?
3. What is the tithe for?
4. What do the ministers and musicians do when the tithe does not come in?
5. Under which priesthood was the tithe revealed?
6. Which priesthood is Jesus the High Priest of?
7. If we want to get God's attention, what can we do?
8. What is an example of an atoning offering?
9. What is an example of a relational offering?

Applications

Ask the Holy Spirit if there are any outstanding tithes and offerings to be given, and give them or make preparations to.

Ask if you have given any vows rashly and not performed them.

Memory Verses

"And all the tithe of the land, whether of the seed of the land, or of the fruit of the tree, is the Lord's: it is holy unto the Lord."
(Leviticus 27:30 KJV)

"Will a man rob God? Yet ye have robbed me. But ye say, Wherein have we robbed thee? In tithes and offerings."
(Malachi 3:8 KJV)

10 Bring ye all the tithes into the storehouse, that there may be meat in mine house, and prove me now herewith, saith the Lord of hosts, if I will not open you the windows of heaven, and pour you out a blessing, that there shall not be room enough to receive it.
11 And I will rebuke the devourer for your sakes, and he shall not destroy the fruits of your ground; neither shall your vine cast her fruit before the time in the field, saith the Lord of hosts.
(Malachi 3:10-11 KJV)

Closing Prayer

   Dearest Father, I thank you that you gave your only begotten Son for me. I thank you that He willingly gave his body and blood for me. In return like my forefathers I bring the tithe into your storehouse that there will be supply for your ministers. I also pray that you ould show me where I can sow my offerings to further Your Kingdom. Help me to be a mature citizen in Your Kingdom and to be a cheerful giver. I ask this in the name of Jesus. Amen.

Sowing and Reaping
Chapter Eight – Study Guide

Opening Prayer

　　Dear Father, You have chosen sowing and reaping as a fundamental law in your creation. Please help me to understand how this works that I may be a successful labourer in Your Kingdom. I ask this in the name of Jesus. Amen

---

The following questions will be answered during study of this chapter:

1. What was the most precious seed that God sowed into the earth?
2. What do you get if you sow to the flesh?
3. What do you get if you sow to the spirit?

The Nature of Sowing and Reaping

It is important for us to understand the concept of sowing and reaping. For the Christian it is a fundamental law of prosperity and also a fact of life for everyone on this Earth.

God could have chosen to give us a life in which we did not have to grow. He could have provided all the money, food, drink, clothes, necessities, and luxuries in great quantities for each soul—unlimited provisions for everybody.

One could say that the Garden of Eden was almost like that; yet even there Adam had to tend and keep the Garden. *(See Genesis. 2:15.)*

God has chosen, however, to give each of us a life that is dependent on sowing and reaping. If you work for someone, then you sow your time and labor and you reap your wages. In business you sow, advertise, and reap; then you close the sale. In evangelism we sow the Word, and we reap when the soul becomes a Christian and grows into a disciple.

Jesus sowed His own life in order to reap our lives!

> *"Verily, verily, I say unto you, except a corn of wheat _____ into the _____ and_____, it abideth alone: but if it die, it _____forth _____ _____."*
> **(John 12:24 KJV)**

Cain and Abel were born to Adam and Eve. Both their jobs involved sowing and reaping.

> *1" And Adam knew Eve his wife; and she conceived, and bare Cain, and said, I have gotten a man from the LORD.*
> *2 And she again bare his brother Abel. And Abel was a _____ ____ _____, but Cain was a _____ ____ ____ _____."*
> **(Genesis 4:1-2 KJV)**

Abel was a shepherd and Cain was a tiller of the ground. Both of their jobs involved sowing and reaping. Cain would sow the seed into the ground and at the time of harvest he would reap the grain.

Abel would tend the sheep, and the rams would impregnate the ewes with their seed. The time of reaping would take place when the lambs would give birth.

In *Matthew Chapter 13* we have a portion of Scripture that describes the purpose, beginning, and end of this world in terms of sowing and reaping.

The kingdom of heaven is likened unto a man which _____ good seed in his field: But while men slept, his enemy came and _____ tares among the wheat, and went his way. *(Read Matthew13:24-43 in the KJV.)*

God is sowing His children, and His enemy, Satan, is sowing his children, but the outcome is good for God's children!

Sowing and reaping are facts of life for everyone on this Earth. It is the law of cause and effect—what you sow you will reap. This has been recognized in other religions, as well; in fact, the Buddhist and Hindu religions refer to it as **Karma**.

Sowing and Reaping Scriptures
> *"Even as I have seen, they that _____ iniquity, and _____ wickedness, reap the same."*
> **(Job 4:8 KJV)**

1. What do you get if you sow iniquity and wickedness? _____

_____

> *5 "They that sow in tears shall reap in _____.*
> *6 He that goeth forth and weepeth, bearing precious seed, shall doubtless come again with rejoicing, bringing his sheaves with him."*
> **(Psalm 126:5-6 KJV)**

2. What do you get if you sow in tears? _____

"The wicked worketh a deceitful work: but to him that soweth _____ shall be a sure reward."
(Proverbs 11:18 KJV)

3. What do you get if you sow righteousness? _____

12 "Sow to yourselves in righteousness, reap in mercy; break up your fallow ground: for it is time to seek the LORD, till he come and rain righteousness upon you."
13 Ye have plowed wickedness, ye have reaped iniquity;"
(Hosea 10:12-13a KJV)

"For he that soweth to his flesh shall of the flesh reap corruption; but he that soweth to the Spirit shall of the Spirit reap life everlasting."
(Galatians 6:8 KJV)

4. What do you get if you sow to the Spirit? _____

We can sum it up with the following Scripture, which tells us that what you give, you will get back in even greater measure. This is true for good or evil and for Christian or non-Christian alike.

"_____, and it will be given to you: good measure, pressed down, shaken together, and running over will be put into your bosom. For with the same measure that you use, it will be measured back to you."
(Luke 6:38 NKJV)

From all the above scriptures God could quite easily have written " Sow, and it will be given to you...."

When we reap, we should remember the poor and our ministers. Do not be misled into believing that all you reap belongs to you.

*"And when ye reap the harvest of your land, thou shalt not wholly reap the corners of thy field, neither shalt thou gather the gleanings of thy harvest. And thou shalt not glean thy vineyard, neither shalt thou gather every grape of thy vineyard; thou shalt **leave them for** _____ _____ _____ : I am the LORD your God."*
(Leviticus 19:9-10 KJV)

5. Who else was the harvest for? _____

*"Speak unto the children of Israel, and say unto them, When ye be come into the land which I give unto you, and shall reap the harvest thereof, then ye shall bring a sheaf of the firstfruits of your harvest **unto the priest**."*
(Leviticus 23:10 KJV)

6. Who else was the harvest for? _____

> *"Let him that is taught in the word communicate unto* _____ _____
> _____ *in all good things.* *Be not deceived; God is not mocked:*
> *for whatsoever a man soweth, that shall he also reap. For he that soweth*
> *to his flesh shall of the flesh reap corruption; but he that soweth to the*
> *Spirit shall of the Spirit reap life everlasting."*
> *(Galatians 6:6-8 KJV)*

7. Who else was the harvest for? _____

Sometimes one can sow, but before it becomes time to reap the seed does not grow or it all gets destroyed. Why is that?

Satan will try and devour what you should be reaping. Make sure that you are giving your tithes and offerings so that the Lord can rebuke the devourer for your sake. Also make sure that you are building God's kingdom through your work and through the church. Always check your motives.

> *"Will a man rob God? Yet ye have robbed me. But ye say, Wherein have*
> *we robbed thee? In tithes and offerings.* *Ye are cursed with a curse: for*
> *ye have robbed me,* *even this whole nation.* *Bring ye all the tithes into*
> *the storehouse,* *that there may be meat in mine house, and prove me now*
> *herewith, saith the LORD of hosts, if I will not open you the windows of*
> *heaven, and pour you out a blessing, that there shall not be room enough*
> *to receive it.* _____ ____ _____ _____ _____
> _____ *for your sakes, and he shall not destroy the fruits*
> *of your ground; neither shall your vine cast her fruit before the time in*
> *the field, saith the LORD of hosts."*
> *(Malachi 3:8-12 KJV)*

> *"Now therefore thus saith the LORD of hosts; Consider your ways. Ye*
> *have sown much, and bring in little; ye eat, but ye have not enough; ye*
> *drink, but ye are not filled with drink; ye clothe you, but there is none*
> *warm; and he that earneth wages earneth wages to put it into a bag with*
> *holes. Thus saith the LORD of hosts;* *Consider your ways.* *Go up to the*
> *mountain, and bring wood, and_____ _____ _____;*
> *and I will take pleasure in it, and I will be glorified, saith the LORD."*
> *(Haggai 1:5-8 KJV)*

8. What were they NOT building? _____

In sowing and reaping let us not forget the effect of rain. Without rain no seed will grow. The rain comes from Heaven. If God withholds it, a nation will have famine; if He gives it, then the seed will grow. God uses famine as one of His judgments.

"For thus saith the Lord GOD; How much more when I send my four sore judgments upon Jerusalem, the sword, and the famine, and the noisome beast, and the pestilence, to cut off from it man and beast?"
(Ezekiel 14:21 KJV)

If you need to prosper, my advice to you is to get on with it. Start sowing, give to good causes, and make sure you are tithing and giving offerings. Look around your home to see if there is something you are not using and give it to someone in need. Many blockages to finances can be unblocked through giving. Don't let your life stagnate.

"He that _____ the wind shall not sow; and he that _____ the clouds shall not reap."
(Ecclesiastes. 11:4 KJV)

Solomon tells us to stop looking at the wind, to get on with it. You don't need to understand how it works. Just know that it does.

Finally, let us not forget Paul's admonition, which declares that you will reap according to how you sow:

6 "But this I say, He which soweth sparingly shall reap also _____; and he which soweth bountifully shall reap also _____.
7 Every man according as he purposeth in his heart, so let him give; not grudgingly, or of necessity: for **God loveth a cheerful giver.**
8 And God is able to make all grace abound toward you; that ye, always having _____ _____ in _____ _____,
may abound to every good work."
(2 Corinthians 9:6-8 KJV)

Reflections
1. What was the most precious seed that God sowed into the earth?
2. What do you get if you sow to the flesh?
3. What do you get if you sow to the Spirit?

Applications
Pray and ask the Holy Spirit to show you what you can sow and to whom you should sow.

Memory Verses

"Verily, verily, I say unto you, Except a corn of wheat fall into the ground and die, it abideth alone: but if it die, it bringeth forth much fruit."
(John 12:24 KJV)

"For he that soweth to his flesh shall of the flesh reap corruption; but he that soweth to the Spirit shall of the Spirit reap life everlasting."
(Galatians 6:8 KJV)

"But this I say, He which soweth sparingly shall reap also sparingly; and he which soweth bountifully shall reap also bountifully."
(2 Corinthians 9:6 KJV)

Closing Prayer

Dear Father, You did not withhold your most precious seed, Jesus, giving Him that I may have life. I ask that not only would I give my money into your Kingdom as seed, but that I would also lay my life down as a living sacrifice for Your World. I ask this in the name of Jesus. Amen.

Entering the Promised Land
Chapter Nine – Study Guide

Opening Prayer

     Dear Father, thank you that you have a hope laid up for me, a Promised Land. Please teach my hands to war, that I can be a valiant soldier in Your Kingdom. I ask this in the name of Jesus. Amen

---

The following questions will be answered during study of this chapter:
1. What is the first prerequisite for obtaining promises from God?
2. What is the second prerequisite for obtaining promises from God?
3. What is the third prerequisite for obtaining promises from God?
4. What is the fourth prerequisite for obtaining promises from God?
5. What is the fifth prerequisite for obtaining promises from God?
6. What is the sixth prerequisite for obtaining promises from God?
7. What is the seventh prerequisite for obtaining promises from God?

Will We Accept the Challenge to Enter the Promised Land?
"How long will you _____ to go and_____ the land which the LORD God of your fathers has_____ you?"
(Joshua. 18:3 NKJV)

On leaving Egypt the children of Israel were given a promise that the LORD would bring them into the Promised Land. It was to be a land flowing with milk and honey.

We have been given similar promises, though not an actual land—yet. We, those who belong to Christ, have been promised the inheritance of the blessings that were given to Abraham. *(See Galatians 3:29.)*

By observing how Israel was able to obtain the Promised Land, we can see a mirrored portrayal of how we should obtain our promises.

> *7 "I have surely seen the oppression of My people who are in Egypt"...*
> **So I have come down to deliver them out of the hand of the Egyptians, and to bring them up from that land to a good and large land, to a land flowing with milk and honey, ...**
> *8 "Come now, therefore, and I will send you to Pharaoh that you may bring My people, the children of Israel, out of Egypt."*
> *(Exodus 3:7-8 NKJV)*

After the children of Israel had come out of Egypt, Moses sent twelve spies, one from each tribe of Israel, to spy out the Promised Land. This is the account of their experience:

> 17 *"Then Moses sent them to spy out the land of Canaan...*
> 27 *"We went to the land where you sent us. It truly _____ _____*
> _____ _____ _____, **and this is its fruit...**
> 30 *Caleb quieted the people before Moses, and said, "Let us go up at once and _____ _____, for we are well able to overcome it."*
> 31 *But the men who had gone up with him said,* **"We are not able to go up against the people, for they are stronger than we."**
> 32 *And they gave the children of Israel a bad report of the land which they had spied out....*
> 2 *And* **all the children of Israel complained against Moses and Aaron..."**
> **(Numbers 13:17-14:2 NKJV)**

After all the miracles that the LORD did in bringing them out of Egypt, most of Israel failed to get into the Promised Land because of unbelief.

Prerequisites for Obtaining God's Promises
The first prerequisite for obtaining promises from God is that you **must** have *faith.*

> 12 *"Take heed, brethren, lest there be in any of you* **an evil heart of unbelief,** *in departing from the living God.*
> 13 *But exhort one another daily, while it is called Today; lest any of you be hardened through the deceitfulness of sin.*
> 14 *For we are made partakers of Christ, if we hold the beginning of our confidence steadfast unto the end;*
> 15 *While it is said, Today if ye will hear his voice, harden not your hearts, as in the provocation.*
> 16 *For some, when they had heard, did provoke: howbeit not all that came out of Egypt by Moses.*
> 17 *But with whom was he grieved forty years? was it not with them that had sinned, whose carcasses fell in the wilderness?*
> 18 *And to whom sware he that they should not enter into his rest, but to them that _____ _____ ?*
> 19 *So we see* **that they could not enter in because of _____."**
> **(Hebrews 3:12-19 KJV)**

1. Why could they not enter into the Promised Land? _____

It was left for Joshua to lead the children into the Promised Land. In the first chapter of Joshua we see the second prerequisite for obtaining promises from God:

2 "Moses My servant is dead. Now therefore, arise, go over this Jordan, you and all this people, to the land which I am giving to them....
*7 Only be strong and very courageous, **that you may** _____*
*___ _____ according to all the law which Moses My servant commanded you; do not turn from it to the right hand or to the left, **that you may prosper wherever you go.***
*8 This Book of the Law shall not depart from your mouth, but you shall meditate in it day and night, that you may observe to do according to all that is written in it. For then **you will make your way prosperous**, and then you will have good success.*
9 Have I not commanded you? Be strong and of good courage; do not be afraid, nor be dismayed, for the LORD your God is with you wherever you go."
(Joshua 1:2-9 NKJV)

Know the Word of God

The second prerequisite is that you must know the Word of God; you must study it and then most important, you must obey it. Success comes from obeying God and knowing His promises.

The Promised Land is a land flowing with milk and honey. This is a beautiful picture, but the Scriptures about the Promised Land are there for more than just art, poetry, beauty, and hope.

When Joshua and the Israelites went into the Promised Land, they were not invited in by the inhabitants of that land. In fact, they had to take the land by force.

Without the action of a force upon us, our lives will stay the same. If you want to obtain a promise of God, you have to apply a force. Life does not just change itself. Sometimes you have to fight in order to obtain your "promised land."

> *"And from the days of John the Baptist until now the kingdom of heaven suffereth violence, and the violent take it by force."*
> ***(Matthew 11:12 KJV)***

> *"_____**the good fight** of faith, _____ _____ **on eternal life**, to which you were also called and have confessed the good confession in the presence of many witnesses."*
> ***(1 Timothy 6:12 NKJV)***

We need to lay hold on eternal life, and we need to lay hold of the Promised Land.

When Joshua entered the Promised Land, he had to fight. If you want to enter your promised land, you will have to fight, as well. You must remember that your enemy does not want you to prosper. Every penny more that you have is a penny less in his kingdom. We have a saying in

England that if you look after the pennies, the pounds will look after themselves.

Satan does not want a shift of economic power into the Kingdom of God, and he will fight you all the way. But we are blessed in that the victory is surely ours; Jesus has been slain so that the blessings would be ours. We need to rise up and take hold of the promises of God. We need to believe them, receive them, and enjoy them.

Faith and Prayer

The third prerequisite for obtaining the promises of God involves applying force by fighting with faith and prayer.

The first battle for the Promised Land was to be against Jericho. Let's take a look at how it was won. *(Read Joshua Chapter 6.)*

> *2 "And the LORD said to Joshua: "See! __ _____ _____ Jericho into your hand, its king, and the mighty men of valor.*
> *3 You shall march around the city, all you men of war; you shall go all around the city once. This you shall do six days.*
> *4 And seven priests shall bear seven trumpets of rams' horns before the ark. But the seventh day you shall march around the city seven times, and the priests shall blow the trumpets.*
> *5 It shall come to pass, when they make a long blast with the ram's horn, and when you hear the sound of the trumpet, that all the people shall shout with a great shout; then the wall of the city will fall down flat. And the people shall go up every man straight before him." ...*
> *20 So the people shouted when the priests blew the trumpets. And it happened when the people heard the sound of the trumpet, and the people shouted with a great shout, that the wall fell down flat. Then the people went up into the city, every man straight before him, and they took the city.*
> *21 And they _____ _____ all that was in the city...."*
> *(Joshua 6:2-21 NKJV)*

Can you imagine the generals who led the troops during the Second World War, Generals Montgomery and Patton, in particular, sitting around a table planning their attacks and saying, "Let's march around the city once for six days and seven times on the seventh day and then blow the trumpets and the walls will fall down."

This is not a normal military strategy. But it does point to an essential strategy for fighting God's battles—*obedience.*

Obedience

The fourth prerequisite for obtaining the promises of God is *obedience.*

The next battle for the children of Israel was a disaster; in fact, it was lost. Why was this? *(See Joshua Chapter 7.)*

> *"Israel has _____, and they have also transgressed My covenant which I commanded them. For they have even taken some of the accursed things, and have both stolen and deceived; and they have also put it among their own stuff.* **"Therefore the children of Israel _____ _____ _____ before their enemies..."**
> *(Joshua 7:11-12 NKJV)*

2. Why could the children of Israel not stand before their enemies? _____
_____

The perpetrators of the sin had to be burned with fire. They had to be sanctified.

Holiness

The fifth prerequisite for obtaining the promises of God is holiness. When we sin, we are not able to obtain the promises. We have to repent, find out what the blockage may be, and remove it.

The inhabitants of Gibeon avoided destruction through craftiness. Let's see what they did: *(Read Joshua Chapter 9.)*

Let us remember that our enemy is as crafty as a serpent. He will try and catch us in legal traps. By making a covenant with the Gibeonites the children of Israel had legally allowed snares in Israel which affected them for hundreds of years. *(See 2 Samuel 21.)*

If they had taken to heart the second prerequisite, which is knowing God's Word, they would not have fallen into the trap.

> *"Take _____ _____ _____, lest you make a covenant with the inhabitants of the land where you are going, lest it be a snare in your midst."*
> *(Exodus 34:12 NKJV)*

Do not allow sin to dwell in your bodies, it will only cause harm.

Ask for the Lord's Counsel

They could also have avoided the trap by using the sixth prerequisite for obtaining the promises of God: *Ask counsel of the LORD.*

Speaking to Christians, Paul says that we can have filthiness of spirit. It is worth noting that Israel allowed unclean people to dwell in their midst through a legal mechanism. It is important that we do not allow unclean spirits to dwell in our midst through legal rights. This can become a snare to our lives. Release yourself from all spiritual oppression through repentance and the cleansing of the blood of Jesus. *(See 1 John 1:7 KJV.)*

> *"Therefore, having these promises, beloved, let us cleanse ourselves from all filthiness of the flesh _____ _____, _____ _____ in the fear of God."*
> **(2 Corinthians 7:1 NKJV)**

Perseverance and Patience

The seventh prerequisite for obtaining the promises of God, your Promised Land, is seen in the following verse:

> *"Joshua made war ____ _____ _____ with all those kings"*
> **(Joshua 11:18 KJV)**.

3. How long was Joshua at war? _____

Therefore, you need to persevere and exercise patience.

> *10 "For God is not unjust to forget your work and labor of love which you have shown toward His name, in that you have ministered to the saints, and do minister.*
> *11 And we desire that each one of you show the _____ _____ to the full assurance of hope _____ _____ _____,*
> *12 that you do not _____ _____, but imitate those who **through faith** _____ _____ **inherit the promises."***
> **(Hebrews 6:10-12 NKJV)**

4. What do we need to get to the full assurance of hope? _____
_____

5. Those we are imitating, did they receive the promises? _____

6. What did they use to inherit the promises? _____
_____

The seventh prerequisite for obtaining the promises of God, therefore, is patience.

Joshua and the children of Israel had seven enemies in the Promised Land. *(See Joshua 3:10.)*

I like to picture these seven nations as enemies to overcome.

In an individual's personal life I am often able to identify the seven enemies as I have indicated below.

This list consists of my own thoughts, and I am sure you could write your own similar list.

The important thing to remember is that identifying your enemies is the first step towards destroying them.

	Your Enemies	**God's Benefits**
Canaanites	Sickness	Health
Hittites	Poverty	Prosperity
Hivites	Fear, Anxiety, War	Peace/Rest
Perizzites	Unbelief	Faith
Girgashites	Sin	Forgiveness
Amorites	Disobedience	Obedience
Jebusites	Uncleanness	Holiness

Reflections

In your own words answer the questions below:

1. What is the first prerequisite for obtaining promises from God?

_____

2. What is the second prerequisite for obtaining promises from God?

_____

3. What is the third prerequisite for obtaining promises from God?

_____

_____

4. What is the fourth prerequisite for obtaining promises from God?

_____

5. What is the fifth prerequisite for obtaining promises from God?

_____

6. What is the sixth prerequisite for obtaining promises from God?

_____

7. What is the seventh prerequisite for obtaining promises from God?

_____

Applications

"Now the whole congregation of the children of Israel assembled together at Shiloh, and set up the tabernacle of meeting there. And the land was subdued before them. But there remained among the children of Israel seven tribes which had not yet received their inheritance. Then Joshua said to the children of Israel:

> *"How long will you neglect to go and possess the land which the LORD God of your fathers has given you?"*
> **(Joshua 18:3b NKJV)**

Read more about the promises of God by studying the Scriptures I've listed here:

Romans 4:19-21
2 Corinthians 1:18-20
Ephesians 1:1-14
Hebrews 4:1-16
Hebrews 6:10-20
Hebrews 9:15-16
James 2:5
2 Peter 1:1-14
1 John 2:25

Memory Verses

"How long will you _____ to go and_____ the land which the LORD God of your fathers has_____ you?"
(Joshua. 18:3b NKJV)

"_____the good fight of faith, _____ _____ on eternal life, to which you were also called and have confessed the good confession in the presence of many witnesses."
(1Timothy 6:12 NKJV)

And from the days of John the Baptist until now the kingdom of heaven suffereth violence, and the violent take it by force.
(Matthew 11:12 KJV)

Closing Prayer

Dear Father, I ask that You would forgive me for neglecting the Promised Land that You have for me, for not receiving the promises by faith, so painfully bought for me by Jesus. Teach me to fight the fight of faith that I may hold the ground bought by my Lord. I ask this in the name of Jesus. Amen.

The Covenants of God
Chapter Ten – Study Guide

The following questions will be answered during study of this chapter:
1. What is a covenant?
2. What is the rainbow?
3. Who did God swear by, when blessing Abraham?
4. How do we receive the promises given to Abraham?

The First Covenant

There are a number of different covenants (or promises) in the Bible. The most significant are those that were given to Noah, Abraham, Moses, and the New Covenant, which came through Jesus.

Simply stated, a covenant is a contract or agreement between two parties.

The first covenant we see in the Bible is the covenant that was made between God and Noah, his seed after him, and every living creature. The nature of this covenant was: "Neither shall all flesh be cut off any more by the waters of a flood; neither shall there any more be a flood to destroy the earth." This was a promise that was made by God, and this promise was without conditions. God also decided to give a token to remind us and Him of this covenant.

12 "And God said, This is the _____ _____ _____ _____ which I make between me and you and every living creature that is with you, for perpetual generations:
13 I do _____ _____ _____ in the cloud, and it shall be for a token of a covenant between me and the earth.
14 And it shall come to pass, when I bring a cloud over the earth, that the bow shall be seen in the cloud:
15 And I will remember my covenant, which is between me and you and every living creature of all flesh; and the waters shall no more become a flood to destroy all flesh."
(Genesis 9:12-15 KJV)

1. What is the token of this covenant? _____

_____

It is interesting to note that the word used for "bow" also means "iris." God is watching it through the iris of His eye.

This covenant set up by God has never been broken!

Covenants and Promises Made to Abraham

These promises that were made to Abraham come from a series of works Abraham was asked to do. At each step the reward Abraham was given becomes greater and greater. Not only were these promises made to him but also to his descendants and his seed, Jesus, from whom we inherited these promises! It is of the utmost importance to understand what our father Abraham received from God, because we are also co-heirs of these precious promises.

As you read these Scriptures, you will see that sometimes Abraham is referred to as Abram. This is because originally he was named Abram, meaning exalted father, and God later changed his name to Abraham, meaning a father of multitudes (nations).

> *1 "Now the LORD had said to Abram: '_____ _____ _____*
> *_____ _____, From your family And from your father's*
> *house, _____ _____ _____ that I will show you.*
> *2 I will make you a great nation; I will bless you And make your name*
> *great; And you shall be a blessing. 3 I will bless those who bless you,*
> *And I will curse him who curses you; And in you all the families of the*
> *earth shall be blessed.'*
> *5 So Abram departed as the LORD had spoken to him..."*
> **(Genesis 12:1-5 NKJV)**

2. What did God ask Abram to do? _____

_____

3. What was the reward for doing it? _____

_____

_____

_____

Abram was asked to leave his home, his country, and his family. This was not a small request from God. Abram was not forced to do it; God asked him to. We have to love God more than anything, more than our homes, our country, and our family. Where would we be if Abram had said, "No"? Did God ask anybody else first; did they turn Him down? The reason I say this is because God is always looking for those who will obey Him. Has God asked you to do something? Then do it. If you don't obey God, the Kingdom of Heaven will not fall down. God will simply find somebody who will obey Him, and they will get their reward.

4. Is somebody else at this moment being asked to do the things you have been asked to do? _____

_____

Abram made a decision to obey God, and he departed as the LORD had directed him to do. The LORD then appeared to Abram and said, "To your descendants I will give this land." Abram had been rewarded for his obedience. God is always faithful to His promises.

> *1 "After these things the word of the LORD came to Abram in a vision, saying, '_____ _____ _____ _____, Abram. I am your shield, your exceedingly great reward.'*
> *2 But Abram said, 'Lord GOD, what will You give me, seeing I go childless....*
> *5 ,,,Look now toward heaven, and count the stars if you are able to number them.' And He said to him, 'So shall your descendants be.'*
> *6 **And he believed in the LORD**, and He accounted it to him for righteousness."*
> *(Genesis 15:1-6 NKJV)*

5. What can stop us obeying God? *(Verse 1)* _____

_____

6. Why did the LORD give Abram righteousness? _____

_____

Here Abram is asked to believe something, ***"Look now toward heaven, and count the stars if you are able to number them." And He said to him, "So shall your descendants be."***

Let us remember that Abram was over seventy-five years of age at this time; he was not a young man. God had said to him that He was his exceedingly great reward. But Abram had something missing. "What will you give me, seeing I go childless?" Nothing material could cover the hole that Abraham felt in his life. So how does God respond? "Look now toward heaven, and count the stars. So shall your descendants be." This must have been a very hard thing for Abram to believe, considering his age. Yet he still believed the Lord.

5 "Then He brought him outside and said, 'Look now toward heaven, and count the stars if you are able to number them.' And He said to him, 'So shall your descendants be.'
*6 And **he believed** in the LORD, and He accounted it to him for righteousness."*
(Genesis 15:5-6 NKJV)

This one act of faith by Abram was rewarded by God giving righteousness to him. Do not underestimate the importance of this event. The whole history of mankind has been shaped by God giving Abram this righteousness. It is sometimes hard to understand, yet this righteousness that was given to Abram was a transferable asset. All of the blessings that were given to Abram we are able to receive through Jesus and the administration of Jesus. *(See Galatians 3:6-14.)*

In the next Scriptures we see God making a covenant with Abram. Abram is asked to walk before God and be blameless. God in turn will multiply his descendants exceedingly, and nations and kings would come from him, and that his name was now to be called Abraham. The sign of this contract was to be circumcision, the cutting away of the foreskin of all males.

1b "I am the Almighty God; _____ before me, and _____
_____ _____.
2 And I will make my covenant between me and thee, and will multiply thee exceedingly....
10 This is my covenant, which ye shall keep, between me and you and thy seed after thee; Every man child among you shall be circumcised...
19 And God said, Sarah thy wife shall bear thee a son indeed; and thou shalt call his name Isaac: and I will establish my covenant with him for an everlasting covenant, and with his seed after him."
(Genesis 17:1b-19 NKJV)

7. What are the two things Almighty God asked Abram to do?
    1. _____
    2. _____

8. What was the 'token' of this covenant given to the male children?

_____

We can see that not only was this covenant made with Abraham, but it was also to be established in his son of promise, Isaac—a son who would be born to a ninety-year-old woman, Sarah.

Just when things seem hard to believe, they often got harder. But Abraham grew strong in faith; he may have started out laughing, but he obtained the son of promise.

So what was the next test for Abraham? He had already left his family, friends, home, and traveled to a foreign country. He obeyed God, lived blamelessly, walked with God, and *believed* God.

What about giving up the one thing he had lacked, hoped for, and received. How about sacrificing his only begotten son? Does this sound familiar? *(Read Genesis Chapter 22.)*

> **1b "God tested Abraham**...
> *2 "Take now your son, your only son Isaac, whom you love, and go to the land of Moriah, and offer him there as a _____ offering....*
> *10 And Abraham stretched out his hand and took the knife _____ _____ his son.*
> *11 But the Angel of the LORD called to him from heaven and said, "Abraham, Abraham!" So he said, "Here I am."*
> *12 And He said, "Do not lay your hand on the lad, or do anything to him; for now I know that you fear God, since* **you have not withheld your son, your only son, from Me...**
> *16b "By Myself I have sworn, says the LORD, because you have done this thing, and have not withheld your son, your only son—*
> *17 "blessing I will bless you, and multiplying I will multiply your descendants as the stars of the heaven and as the sand which is on the seashore; and your descendants shall possess the gate of their enemies.*
> *18 "In your seed all the nations of the earth shall be blessed, because you have obeyed My voice."*
> **(Genesis 22:1b-18 NKJV)**

Abraham did not waste time; he left early in the morning. Imagine what a night that must have been. Did Abraham toss and turn all night? Something monumental was to happen; a definite deadline was coming up. Three days it took to travel to the appointed place of sacrifice, and that was plenty of time to change one's mind. Was it God who spoke, or was it not God who spoke?

We don't know what was going through Abraham's mind. He believed he was to be the father of nations, yet God was asking him to sacrifice his son, Isaac. How could he sacrifice the son through whom the promises were to come? The only answer was that God must be able to raise him from the dead.

This we know Abraham thought, because it says so in *Hebrews 11:19*:

> *17 "By faith Abraham, when he was tried, offered up Isaac: and he that had received the promises offered up his only begotten son,*
> *18 Of whom it was said, That in Isaac shall thy seed be called:*
> *19* **Accounting that God was able** _____ _____ _____, _____
> **even** _____ _____ _____; *from whence also he received him in a figure"*
> **(Hebrews 11:17-19 KJV)**

This testing of Abraham's faith and obedience, I believe, goes far beyond his own situation.

I believe this was a proving of mankind. Thus, when Jesus said that He was to be raised from the dead on the third day, the faith of Jesus could not be refuted. What I mean is that Satan could not question the validity of the faith employed by the son of man by saying "It is not in mankind to be able to believe that a man could be raised from the dead!" The Father could quite easily say, "Look at my friend Abraham; he believed I could raise Isaac from the dead!" It was not only Jesus that had faith to rise from the dead.

God was so moved by Abraham's willingness to sacrifice his only begotten son and his willingness to believe that God was able to raise him from the dead that He decided to bless Abraham.

> *16 "By _____ I have sworn, says the LORD, because you have done this thing, and have not withheld your son, your only son—*
> *17 "blessing I will bless you, and multiplying I will multiply your descendants as the stars of the heaven and as the sand which is on the seashore; and your descendants shall possess the gate of their enemies.*
> *18 "In your seed all the nations of the earth shall be blessed, because you have obeyed My voice."*
> *(Genesis 22:16-18 NKJV)*

9. Who did God swear by? _____

10. What did Abraham not withhold? _____

11. What did God promise him in return? _____
_____
_____
_____

The Promises

"Blessing I will bless you." This phrase is so small, yet so **huge.** The ramifications stretch to every believer who has lived after Abraham. This is because this blessing was passed as an inheritance through Isaac and Jacob/Israel and to the Gentiles through Jesus.

> *"In Christ Jesus the blessing of Abraham might come to the Gentiles, so that we would receive the promise of the Spirit through faith."*
> *(Galatians 3:14 NASB)*

12. In whom are we receiving the blessing of Abraham? _____

13. From whom are we receiving the promise of the Spirit? _____

14. What are we using to receive the promises given to Abraham?

_____

If I promise to bless you by saying, "Blessing, I will bless you," then I can do so to the limit of everything I possess.

If a king were to bless you by saying, "Blessing, I will bless you," then the limit of blessing will be that which the king possesses.

Similarly, when Almighty God says, "Blessing, I will bless you." What is the limit of this blessing? We can see from the verse of Galatians quoted above that included in what God possesses is His Spirit. This is linked to the promise that was given to Abraham as part of the blessings.

When trying to find the limits of the blessings given to Abraham, I try to imagine what is the most precious thing I know God has? Of course that has to be His Son, Jesus.

> *"He who did not spare His own Son, but delivered Him over for us all, how will He not also with Him freely give us all things?"*
> **(Romans 8:32 NKJV)**

We can see that God has held nothing back in blessings, and He has said that with Him, that is, Jesus, He will freely give us all things.

> *34 "And he said, I am Abraham's servant.*
> *35 And the LORD hath blessed my master greatly; and he is become great: and he hath given him flocks, and herds, and silver, and gold, and menservants, and maidservants, and camels, and asses."*
> **(Genesis 24:34-35 KJV)**

> *"And Abraham was old, and well stricken in age: and the LORD had blessed Abraham _____ _____ _____."*
> **(Genesis 24:1 KJV)**

15. What was the extent to which Abraham was blessed? _____

The whole universe, the heavens and the Earth, are governed by laws. God's justice decrees that righteousness is observed from the heavenly perspective at all times. Even God limits himself at times by means of His Word, thereby giving us stability.

We see this mirrored in Scripture when King Darius could not undo a law that he made; therefore, he condemned Daniel to the lions' den.

Even though King Darius did not want Daniel to be put into the lions' den, he could not stop it, because he had to enforce the law that he had decreed. *(See Daniel Chapter 6.)*

Even God cannot do what He wants to, when He limits himself by His own Word. This is why the human soul has free will on Earth. This is why we have the freedom to kill and to love; we have the power of choice. Of course, it is not God's will for us to murder, but it is His will for us to love. Why do we pray, "Thy will be done on earth as it is in heaven," if His will is being done?

Has God given himself the freedom to bless anybody whenever He wants to? I don't know, but what I do know is that He has blessed Abraham and his seed, which is Jesus, and through Jesus He has blessed me!

Is this in Scripture, and can I be blessed as well?

> *13 "Christ has redeemed us from the curse of the law, having become a curse for us (for it is written, "Cursed is everyone who hangs on a tree"),*
> *14 **that the blessing of Abraham might come upon the Gentiles in Christ Jesus, that we might receive the promise of the Spirit through faith.***
> *15 Brethren, I speak in the manner of men: Though it is only a man's covenant, yet if it is confirmed, **no one annuls or adds to it.***
> *16 Now to Abraham and his Seed were the promises made. He does not say, "And to seeds," as of many, but as of one, "And to your Seed," who is Christ.*
> *17 And this I say, that the law, which was four hundred and thirty years later, **cannot annul the covenant** that was confirmed before by God in Christ, that it should make the promise of no effect.*
> *18 For **if the inheritance is of the law, it is no longer of promise;** but God gave it to Abraham by promise.*
> *19 What purpose then does the law serve? It was added because of transgressions, till the Seed should come to whom the promise was made; and it was appointed through angels by the hand of a mediator.*
> *20 Now a mediator does not mediate for one only, but God is one.*
> *21 Is the law then against the promises of God? Certainly not! For if there had been a law given which could have given life, truly righteousness would have been by the law.*
> *22 But the Scripture has confined all under sin, **that the promise by faith in Jesus Christ might be given to those who believe.***
> *23 But before faith came, we were kept under guard by the law, kept for the faith which would afterward be revealed.*
> *24 Therefore the law was our tutor to bring us to Christ, that we might be justified by faith.*
> *25 But after faith has come, we are no longer under a tutor.*
> *26 For you are all sons of God through faith in Christ Jesus.*
> *27 For as many of you as were baptized into Christ have put on Christ."*
> ***(Galatians 3:13-27 NKJV)***

It seems to me that God has placed a "trust fund" on the Earth for His children. This trust fund was set up by God, through Abraham's works, to be received by Jesus and then inherited by the rest of the children of God.

> *3 "Blessed be the God and Father of our Lord Jesus Christ, **who has blessed us with** _____ _____ _____ **in the heavenly places in Christ…***
> *5 having predestined us to adoption as sons by Jesus Christ to Himself."*
> ***(Ephesians 1:3-5 NKJV)***

16. How many spiritual blessings do we have? _____

And for this reason He is the Mediator of the new covenant, by means of death, for the redemption of the transgressions under the first covenant, that those who are **called *may receive the promise of the eternal inheritance.*** *(See Hebrews 9:15.)*

I would also go so far as to say that it is because of this promise to Abraham that we are legally entitled to pray for things. This is why we can pray for them in faith, because they have already been paid for.

> *21 "Jesus answered and said unto them, Verily I say unto you, ___ ____ _____ ____, and doubt not, ye shall not only do this which is done to the fig tree, but also if ye shall say unto this mountain, Be thou removed, and be thou cast into the sea; it shall be done.*
> *22 And _____ _____, whatsoever ye shall ask in prayer, believing, ye shall receive."*
> ***(Matthew 21:21-22 KJV)***

In *Matthew 21:2*, Jesus frames the extent of what we can pray for.

17. What things did Jesus say we could pray for? _____

18. To reinitiate what two things does it say in *Hebrews 6:12* that we need to receive the promises of God?

    1. _____
    2. _____

Reflections

1. What is a covenant?
2. What is the rainbow?
3. Who did God swear by, when blessing Abraham?
4. How do we receive the promises given to Abraham?

Memory Verses

"In Christ Jesus the blessing of Abraham might come to the Gentiles, so that we would receive the promise of the Spirit through faith."
(Galatians 3:14 NASB)

"He who did not spare His own Son, but delivered Him up for us all, how will He not also with Him freely give us all things?"
(Romans 8:32 NKJV)

*3 "Blessed be the God and Father of our Lord Jesus Christ, **who has blessed us with all spiritual blessings in the heavenly places in Christ...** 5 having predestined us to adoption as sons by Jesus Christ to Himself."*
(Ephesians 1:3 & 5 NKJV)

*16b **"By myself I have sworn,** says the LORD, because you have done this thing, and have not withheld your son, your only son—*
17 "blessing I will bless you, and multiplying I will multiply your descendants as the stars of the heaven and as the sand which is on the seashore; and your descendants shall possess the gate of their enemies.
18 "In your seed all the nations of the earth shall be blessed, because you have obeyed My voice."
(Genesis 22:16-18 NKJV)

Closing Prayer

Dear Father, thank you for the covenant you made with Abraham my father. I ask that you would give me the faith and patience needed to receive from the blessings you gave him and passed to me through the work of Jesus. I ask you for these things in the name of Jesus. Amen.

The Inheritance
Chapter Eleven – Study Guide

Opening Prayer

     Dear Jesus, thank you for dying for me, so that I am able to inherit the blessings given to Abraham and to his seed, **yourself,** my Lord. Help me to understand the fullness of this inheritance and how to draw from it to help build **Your Kingdom**. I ask this in your name, Jesus. Amen.

The following questions will be answered during study of this chapter:
1. When does a testament come into force?
2. What was given to Jesus after He died?
3. Who is the guarantee of our inheritance?
4. Who will not inherit the Kingdom of God?

Obtaining Inheritance

When the Israelites were going into the Promised Land, they were told that it was going to be their inheritance. But they had to fight for it. The land was to be divided up by lot and then passed through to the next generations through the tribes and families.

> *"And you shall divide the land by lot _____ _____ _____ among your families; to the larger you shall give a larger inheritance, and to the smaller you shall give a smaller inheritance; there everyone's inheritance shall be whatever falls to him by lot. You shall inherit according to the tribes of your fathers."*
> *(Numbers 33:54 NKJV)*

The land that the Israelites were to inherit was flowing with milk and honey; in fact, it was such a blessing that there was a real possibility of having no poor people there at all!

> *"Except when there may be no poor among you; for the LORD will greatly bless you in the land which the LORD your God is _____ _____ to possess as _____ _____."*
> *(Deuteronomy 15:4 NKJV)*

Now as we know from an earthly point of view, if we are to inherit something, someone has to die. So who died, and what did we inherit?

Let us read the following Scripture carefully:

11 "But Christ came as High Priest... 12b with His own blood He entered the Most Holy Place once for all, having obtained eternal redemption...
*15 And for this reason **He is the Mediator of the new covenant,** by*
_____ ____ _____, **for the redemption of the transgressions under the first** *covenant, that those who are called* **may receive the** _____ **of the** _____

_____.

16 For where there is a testament, there must also of necessity be the death of the testator.
17 For a testament is in force after men are dead, since it has no power at all while the testator lives"
(Hebrews 9:11-17 NKJV).

1. When does a testament come into force? _____

2. Who died? _____

3. Who has received the eternal inheritance? _____

Jesus died; He was crucified on the cross. But this was a travesty of justice. The wages of sin is death, yet Jesus had not sinned. Therefore, God intervened and raised Him from the dead.

But the plain fact is that He did die. Therefore, His property, whether physical or spiritual, can be legally passed on as an inheritance. A last will and testament is in force after a person is dead.

It is appointed for a man to die once and then the judgment. *(See Hebrews 9:27.)*

What was Jesus' judgment?

Let's see what He told His disciples after He was raised from the dead:

16 "Then the eleven disciples went away into Galilee, to the mountain which Jesus had appointed for them.
17 When they saw Him, they worshiped Him; but some doubted.
18 And Jesus came and spoke to them, saying, "_____ _____ **has been given to Me in**_____ **and on** _____ "*
(Matthew 28:16-18 NKJV).

4. What was the judgment given to Jesus? _____
_____

All authority in Heaven and on Earth has been given to Jesus. That's quite a reward. Jesus died and His judgment was given to Him. The Father gave Him all authority in Heaven and on Earth. One day we will all have to stand before the Father for our judgment. Therefore, make sure you receive a reward and not condemnation.

"Saying with a loud voice: "Worthy is the Lamb who was slain to receive _____ and _____ and _____, And _____ and _____ and _____ and _____!"
(Revelation 5:12 NKJV)

In Revelation we see in more detail what Jesus received.

5. What did He receive? _____

_____

"Knowing that from the Lord you will receive the reward of the inheritance; for you serve the Lord Christ."
(Colossians 3:24 NKJV)

6. Who do we receive the reward of the inheritance from? _____

_____

Having been raised from the dead, Jesus is in the unusual position of being the administrator of His own estate, and He is able to choose who He gives His belongings to.

Those who serve the Lord Christ receive their inheritance under the administration of Jesus.

Does Scripture really say that I have a part in this inheritance?

*"And for this reason He is the Mediator of the new covenant, by means of death, for the redemption of the transgressions under the first covenant, **that those who are called may receive the promise of the eternal inheritance."***
(Hebrews 9:15 NKJV)

7. Who will receive the promise of the eternal inheritance? _____

_____

*"Giving thanks to the _____ who has qualified us to be partakers of the **inheritance** of the saints in the light."*
(Colossians 1:12 NKJV)

8. Who has qualified us? _____

> 11 "In Him also we have obtained an inheritance...
> 13b   having believed, you were sealed with the _____ _____ of promise,
> 14 **who is the guarantee of our inheritance** until the redemption of the purchased possession, to the praise of His glory.
> 15 Therefore I also, after I heard of your faith in the Lord Jesus and your love for all the saints,
> 16 do not cease to give thanks for you, making mention of you in my prayers:
> 17 that the God of our Lord Jesus Christ, the Father of glory, may give to you the spirit of wisdom and revelation in the knowledge of Him,
> 18 the eyes of your understanding being enlightened; that you may know what is the hope of His calling, **what are the riches of the glory of His inheritance in the saints."**
> **(Ephesians 1:11-18 NKJV)**

9. Who is the guarantee of our inheritance? _____

> "To open their eyes, in order to turn them from darkness to light, and from the power of Satan to God, **that they may receive** forgiveness of **sins and an inheritance** among those who are sanctified by faith in Me."
> **(Acts 26:18 NKJV)**

10. Who are those that receive the inheritance? _____

11. What is it that sanctifies them? _____

If you are sanctified by faith in Jesus, then you qualify as a partaker of the inheritance.

So as Isaac received an inheritance from his father, Abraham, so we receive our inheritance from our Father through Jesus, our Lord.

12. What have we inherited from Jesus, and how do we receive it? _____

_____

> "Are they not all ministering spirits sent forth to minister for those who will **inherit salvation?"**
> **(Hebrews 1:14 NKJV)**

13. What do we inherit? _____

13 "In Him you also trusted, after you heard the word of truth, the gospel of your salvation; in whom also, having believed, you were sealed with the Holy Spirit of promise,
14 who is the guarantee of our inheritance until the redemption of the purchased possession, to the praise of His glory."
(Ephesians 1:13-14 NKJV)

14. What do we inherit? _____

*"He who overcomes shall **inherit all things**, and I will be his God and he shall be My son."*
(Revelation 21:7 NKJV)

15. What do we inherit? _____

*"Not returning evil for evil or reviling for reviling, but on the contrary blessing, knowing that you were called to this, that you may **inherit a blessing**."*
(1 Peter 3:9 NKJV)

16. What do we inherit? _____

*"That you do not become sluggish, but imitate those who through faith and patience **inherit the promises**."*
(Hebrews 6:12 NKJV)

17. What do we inherit? _____

*"Then the King will say to those on His right hand, 'Come, you blessed of My Father, **inherit the kingdom** prepared for you from the foundation of the world.'"*
(Matthew 25:34 NKJV)

18. What do we inherit? _____

*"Blessed are the meek, For they shall **inherit the earth**."*
(Matthew 5:5 NKJV)

19. What do we inherit? _____

*"And everyone who has left houses or brothers or sisters or father or mother or wife or children or lands, for My name's sake, shall receive a hundredfold, and **inherit eternal life**."*
(Matthew 19:29 NKJV)

20. What do we inherit? _____

> *"That I may cause those who love me to **inherit wealth, that I may fill their treasuries"***
> *(Proverbs 8:21 NKJV)*

21. What do we inherit? _____

> *"Wait on the LORD, And keep His way, And He shall exalt you to **inherit the land;** When the wicked are cut off, you shall see it."*
> *(Psalm 37:34 NKJV)*

22. What do we inherit? _____

By reading the list of Scriptures above, we see that we inherit from Jesus salvation and the Holy Spirit. Now the Holy Spirit is the deposit for the rest of the inheritance. As executor of His own testament, Jesus is able to distribute the inheritance in whatever ways He wishes. Yet, He seems to give us this grace sometimes according to our works.

For instance, in *1 Peter 3:9*, we see that we will inherit a blessing in return for blessing others.

> *"He _____ _____ shall inherit all things."*
> *(Revelation 21:7 NKJV)*

> *"Blessed are _____ _____ for they shall inherit the earth."*
> *(Matthew 5:5 KJV)*

> *"Everyone who has left houses or brothers or sisters or father or mother or wife or children or lands, for My name's sake, shall receive a hundredfold, and inherit _____ _____."*
> *(Matthew 19:29 NKJV)*

We have a wise God, a Father who puts our growth in character above our growth in possessions.

Paul prays that we would be able to know the fullness of our inheritance. *(See Ephesians 1:18.)*

In *Hebrews Chapter 6*, we see that faith and patience, also, are needed to inherit the promises. We don't just become Christians, and then suddenly inherit everything.

Patience is needed because it takes time for the physical to manifest the spiritual.

"You have put all things in subjection under his feet." For in that He put all in subjection under him, He left nothing that is not put under him. **But now we do not _____ _____ _____ _____ put under him."**
(Hebrews 2:8 NKJV)

Though everything has been put in subjection under Jesus' feet, we do not yet see this reality. But we are heading towards a time when it will be. The Earth will be completely under the feet of Jesus; in fact, we read in Scripture that Jesus will come and reign on Earth for a thousand years. *(See Revelation Chapter 20.)*

Let us also be wary that we do not fall short by not inheriting that which Jesus has for us.

Let us listen to the warnings given by Paul:

18 "But if ye be led of the Spirit, ye are not under the law.
19 Now the works of the flesh are manifest, which are these; Adultery, fornication, uncleanness, lasciviousness,
20 Idolatry, witchcraft, hatred, variance, emulations, wrath, strife, seditions, heresies,
*21 Envyings, murders, drunkenness, revellings, and such like: of the which I tell you before, as I have also told you in time past, that **they which do such things _____ _____ inherit the kingdom of God."***
(Galatians 5:18-21 KJV)

*"Know ye not that **the unrighteous shall not inherit the kingdom of God."***
(1 Corinthians. 6:9a KJV)

17 "But with whom was he grieved forty years? was it not with them that had sinned, whose carcases fell in the wilderness?
18 And to whom sware he that they should not enter into his rest, but to _____ _____ _____ _____?
*19 **So we see that they could not enter in because of unbelief"***
(Hebrews 3:17-19 KJV)

We started this study on the inheritance in the Book of Numbers, so let's go back there:

54 "'And you shall divide the land by lot as an inheritance among your families... You shall inherit according to the tribes of your fathers.
*55 **But if you do not _____ _____ the inhabitants of the land from before you, then it shall be that those whom you let remain shall be irritants in your eyes and thorns in your sides,** and they shall harass you in the land where you dwell.*
*56 **Moreover it shall be that I will do to you as I thought to do to them'"***
(Numbers 33:54-56 NKJV)

Although the inheritance was marked out for them by lot, they had to drive out the inhabitants of the land. If they would not have driven out the inhabitants of the land, the people there would have become thorns in their sides.

Brothers and sisters, you have to fight and contend for your inheritance. Scripture says that you are to fight the good fight of faith, and that our inheritance of the promises would come through faith and patience.

I believe that the inhabitants of the land that we have to drive out are the sins that are inside of us. It is sin that stops us from inheriting the promises of God. As a result, instead of receiving a blessing, we receive punishment. When we allow sin to remain, then we are partakers of the punishment. *(See Numbers 33:56.)* When we drive the sin out, we inherit the land. Look at how often the inheritance is given due to good character. Pride is sin; the opposite of pride is meekness.

23. What happens to the meek? _____
(See Matthew 5:5.)

Are you going to remain in poverty? Are you going to remain in sickness? Are you defeated?

You must fight the good fight of faith. Don't let go. Resist the devil and he will flee. The devil tries to steal your inheritance. He lies to you, and tells you that you are not worthy to receive from God.

Well, don't worry about that, for it's true that you are not worthy. You didn't need to be. It is the Lamb of God who is worthy. All you have to do is do your best and fight. Don't settle for the status quo in life. Stagnation is unworthy of the Lamb. He would rather have us hot or cold.

Paul tells us to pray, that we would understand the riches of the glory of the inheritance. Why do we not clearly understand it?

> *"These are also proverbs of Solomon, which the men of Hezekiah king of Judah copied out. It is the glory of God to conceal a thing: but the honour of kings is to search out a matter."*
> **(Proverbs 25:1-2 KJV)**

Sometimes God plays "hide and seek" with us. In other words, He says, "If you want it, come and find it." He knows that those who do not believe will not come looking. Those who believe the Scriptures and have patience will look and they will find. God typically takes each of His children and puts them through a training program. When you have passed these tests, you will receive more of His inheritance.

"_____ is the man that endureth temptation: for when he is tried, he shall receive the _____ _____ _____, which the **Lord hath promised** *to them that love him."*
(James 1:12 KJV)

24. What happens to the man that endureth temptation? _____
_____

25. What happens to the man that is tried and loves Jesus?_____
_____

Reflections
1. When does a testament come into force?
2. What was given to Jesus after He died?
3. Who is the guarantee of our inheritance?
4. Who will not inherit the Kingdom of God?

Applications
Make a list of everything the scriptures tell us that we can inherit.
Ask Father to release them to you in Jesus' name.

Memory Verses
"Giving thanks unto the Father, which hath made us meet to be partakers of the inheritance of the saints in light:"
(Colossians 1:12 KJV)

"Blessed are the meek: for they shall inherit the earth."
(Matthew 5:5 KJV)

"Knowing that of the Lord ye shall receive the reward of the inheritance: for ye serve the Lord Christ."
(Colossians 3:24 KJV)

Closing Prayer

Dear Father. I pray *17 That the God of our Lord Jesus Christ, the Father of glory, may give unto you the spirit of wisdom and revelation in the knowledge of him: 18 The eyes of your understanding being enlightened; that ye may know what is the hope of his calling, and* **what the riches of the glory of his inheritance in the saints,** *19 And what is the exceeding greatness of his power to usward who believe, according to the working of his mighty power, 20 Which he wrought in Christ, when he raised him from the dead, and set him at his own right hand in the heavenly places, (continued) 21 Far above all principality, and power, and might, and dominion, and every name that is named, not only in this world, but also in that which is to come: 22 And hath put all things under his feet, and gave him to be the head over all things to the church, 23 Which is his body, the fulness of him that filleth all in all.*

(Ephesians 1:17-23 KJV)

I ask this in the name of Jesus. Amen.

Faith
Chapter Twelve – Study Guide

Opening Prayer
　　Dear Father, I know that without faith it is impossible to please You. I really, really want to please You, so please give me grace that I may learn, understand and grow in faith. I ask this in the name of Jesus. Amen.

The following questions will be answered during study of this chapter:
1. What is faith?
2. How does faith come?
3. What type of money is faith?
4. What animal uses faith?
5. How to increase faith?

Understanding Faith
God has asked us not to be slothful, but followers of them who through faith and patience inherit the promises. Let us not be slothful, therefore, in understanding faith.

> *That ye be not slothful,*
> *but followers of them who through _____ and _____*
> *inherit the promises.*
> *(Hebrews 6:12 KJV)*

Faith is one of the big three subjects to be found in the Bible. These three are: faith, hope, and love, with love being the greatest. They are like the primary colors of yellow, blue, and red. All other colors are mixtures of these three. Likewise, all the subjects contained in the Bible could be said to be mixtures of these three great subjects.

　　"And now abide _____, _____,_____, these three; but the greatest of these is love."
　　(1 Corinthians 13:13 NKJV)

King David had three mighty men, and these three topics are God's "mighty men."

Faith Is "Spiritual Money"

The simplest way I can think of to describe faith is to say that faith is spiritual money. In the physical plane when you want to buy something, you have to pay for it with money. As we discussed previously *(See Chapter 4)*, a nation's currency is in effect based on the authority that is promised by the governing bodies. (For example, British Sterling Notes are governed by the Bank of England that promises to pay the bearer of the notes.)

In the spiritual plane, when you want to pray for something, you have to pay for it with faith. You need authority from the Kingdom of Heaven to present with your request, and this is the "spiritual money" that is known as faith.

> *"For whatever is born of God overcomes the world. And this is the victory that has overcome the world—_____ _____."*
> **(1 John 5:4 NKJV)**

1. What is it that causes us to overcome the world? _____

> *"But without _____ it is _____ to please Him, for he who comes to God must believe that He is, and that He is a rewarder of those who diligently seek Him."*
> **(Hebrews 11:6 NKJV)**

2. What do you need to please God? _____

3. Is it possible to please God without this? _____

When we "buy" something in prayer, we are required to state what we want, and then we must believe that we have received it.

> *"And whatever things you ask in prayer,_____, you will receive."*
> **(Matthew 21:22 NKJV)**

Faith is Believing

So faith is believing. Later, we will see that it is much more than simply believing. Having not yet seen the answer to a particular prayer, we have been asked by God to believe that it will happen. This belief in the unseen is faith.

> *"Now faith is _____ _____ of things hoped for, the _____ of things not seen."*
> **(Hebrews 11:2 KJV)**

4. What type of material is faith?_____

Faith is the power to make prayer effective. This spiritual power is given to us as a gift from God and also as fruit from the presence of the Holy Spirit. (Later in this chapter we shall look into this more.)

I have often wondered why God has chosen believing to be the key to releasing power. The best answer I can think of is that in the beginning Eve chose to believe the snake in the Garden of Eden over the words of God. She chose to believe Satan rather than God. Now we are called to believe God rather than Satan before we can enter into the glorious Kingdom of Christ.

Life is a choice. Who are we going to believe, God or Satan?

Faith is a Power

I can also see that "faith" as a power is a fundamental building block of this universe.

> *"By faith we understand that the worlds were framed by the word of God, so that the things which are seen were not made of things which are visible."*
> *(Hebrews 11:3 NKJV)*

What has not yet been appreciated by most is that we are to be children of God who possess the attributes of our Father. One of His attributes involves being creative through the autonomous power of faith.

Just as we need to be good stewards with our money, we need to be good stewards of our faith. Being good stewards over money does not prevent us from using our money as we will, for either good or selfish purposes. In the same manner, God wants us to grow in power, but this growth needs to be in check with our spiritual maturity, due to the autonomous nature of faith and power.

When Jesus was in the Garden of Gethsemane, He said that He could ask His Father for twelve legions of angels and that the Father would provide it for Him. Yet, we also know that this would have been against the will of God. Therefore, Jesus did not ask for it, even though He knew it would have been granted if He had!

> *53 "Or do you think that I cannot now pray to My Father, and _____ _____ _____ _____ with more than twelve legions of angels?*
> *54 How then could the Scriptures be fulfilled, that it must happen thus?"*
> *(Matthew 26:53-54 NKJV)*

Likewise, by faith Peter was able to stand on the water with Jesus, but one moment later, he was sinking. The will of God had not changed within that moment. What had changed was the faith that Peter possessed. So whether God wanted him to stand or sink was not the key factor in whether he stood or sank.

> *29 "So He said, 'Come.' And when Peter had come down out of the boat _____ _____ _____ _____ _____ to go to Jesus.*
> *30 But when he saw that the wind was boisterous, he was afraid; and beginning to sink he cried out, saying, 'Lord, save me!'"*
> **(Matthew 14:29-30 NKJV)**

There is a neutral aspect involved with the power of faith, just as there is with money. It can be spent for good or evil. In fact, faith in the wrong hands can be used in witchcraft.

Sometimes when people are poor, it is not good enough just to give them money. It is far better to teach them "how" to create wealth.

In the same manner, we can see from Jesus' ministry that He tried to encourage the growth of belief/faith, rather than just using His own faith to heal people.

> *17b "Teacher, I brought You my son, who has a mute spirit.*
> *18 And wherever it seizes him, it throws him down; he foams at the mouth, gnashes his teeth, and becomes rigid. So I spoke to Your disciples, that they should cast it out, but they could not.'*
> *19 He answered him and said, '_____ _____ _____, how long shall I be with you? How long shall I bear with you? Bring him to Me.'*
> *20 Then they brought him to Him. And when he saw Him, immediately the spirit convulsed him, and he fell on the ground and wallowed, foaming at the mouth. 21 So He asked his father, 'How long has this been happening to him?' And he said, 'From childhood.*
> *22 And often he has thrown him both into the fire and into the water to destroy him. But if You can do anything, have compassion on us and help us."*
> *23 Jesus said to him, '**If you can believe**, _____ _____ _____ _____ _____ _____ ___ _____ ,*
> *24 Immediately the father of the child cried out and said with tears,* **'Lord, I believe; help my unbelief!'**
> **(Mark 9:17b-24 NKJV)**

> *27 "When Jesus departed from there, two blind men followed Him, crying out and saying, 'Son of David, have mercy on us!'*
> *28b .... And Jesus said to them, 'Do you believe that I am able to do this?' They said to Him, 'Yes, Lord.'*
> *29 Then He touched their eyes, saying, **'According to your faith let it be to you.'***
> *30 And their eyes were opened."*
> **(Matthew 9:27-30 NKJV)**

5. What caused the blind men's eyes to be opened? _____

> 20 "And suddenly, a woman who had a flow of blood for twelve years came from behind and touched the hem of His garment.
> 21 For she said to herself, 'If only I may touch His garment, I shall be made well.'
> 22 But Jesus turned around, and when He saw her He said, 'Be of good cheer, daughter; _____ _____ **has made you well.**' And the woman was made well from that hour."
> **(Matthew 9:20-22 NKJV)**

6. What caused the woman to be made well? _____

> "Then they came to Him, bringing a paralytic who was carried by four men. And when they could not come near Him because of the crowd, they uncovered the roof where He was. So when they had broken through, they let down the bed on which the paralytic was lying. **When Jesus** _____ _____ _____, He said to the paralytic, 'Son, your sins are forgiven you.'"
> **(Mark 2:3-5 NKJV)**

7. What moved Jesus to forgive the paralytic's sins? _____

> 8 "And in Lystra a certain man without strength in his feet was sitting, a cripple from his mother's womb, who had never walked.
> 9 This man heard Paul speaking. **Paul, observing him intently and** _____ _____ _____ _____ _____ _____ _____ _____,
> 10 said with a loud voice, 'Stand up straight on your feet!' And he leaped and walked."
> **(Acts 14:8-10 NKJV)**

8. What moved Paul to command the healing of the cripple? _____

Great Works Achieved Through Faith

In the Book of Hebrews we read about many of the great works that have been achieved through faith. The following passage discusses some of these works:

(See Hebrews 10:38-12:2.) It would be good for your faith to study each of the people listed.

As spiritual people, we are still learning how to be like God. Jesus said that with faith no bigger than a mustard seed we will be able to move mountains, and He clearly stated that nothing is impossible for us.

17 "Then Jesus answered and said, 'O faithless and perverse generation, how long shall I be with you? How long shall I bear with you? Bring him here to Me.'
18 And Jesus rebuked the demon, and it came out of him; and the child was cured from that very hour.
19 Then the disciples came to Jesus privately and said, 'Why could we not cast it out?'
20 So Jesus said to them, 'Because of your unbelief; for assuredly, I say to you, if you have _____ _____ _____ _____
_____ *, you will say to this mountain, "Move from here to there," and it will move; and nothing will be impossible for you.'"*
(Matthew 17:17-20 NKJV)

This type of faith that enables us to move mountains is not yet common to the people of God. Yet Jesus says it is possible. We see glimpses of Jesus' abilities in certain ministries, but we don't see anybody walking in the fullness of Jesus' faith—yet. Jesus demonstrated His faith by walking on water, changing water into wine, multiplying fish, great multiple healings, etc.

We have His example; now we need to find the faith.

Remember, it has taken scientists thousands of years to develop nuclear bombs, bombs of such *great power*. Before the first atomic bomb was exploded they knew it was possible, but even so it had never happened before.

Likewise, the power to move a mountain is enormous; yet we know it is possible. For us to receive great faith is obviously on God's heart. Can you hear the disappointment in Jesus' following words?

> *"Nevertheless, when the Son of Man comes,* _____ _____ _____ _____ _____ *on the earth?"*
> *(Luke 18:8 NKJV)*

I think we should take this verse to heart, forget any negative aspects that circulate about the message of faith, and understand and obtain the faith of the Kingdom of God.

If the nuclear scientists had been so negative, they would not have found the power that ended the Second World War.

When we come to Christ, we are saved through faith. That initial deposit of faith is given to us as a gift.

> *"For by grace you have been* _____ _____ _____,
> *and that not of yourselves; it is the gift of God."*
> *(Ephesians 2:8 NKJV)*

"We are bound to thank God always for you, brethren, as it is fitting, **because your _____ _____ exceedingly,** *and the love of every one of you all abounds toward each other."*
(2 Thessalonians 1:3 NKJV)

9. Can we grow our faith? _____

4 *"There are diversities of gifts, but the same Spirit....*
7 *But the manifestation of the Spirit is given to each one for the profit of all:*
8 *for to one is given the word of wisdom through the Spirit...*
9 to another faith *by the same Spirit....*
11 *But one and the same Spirit works all these things,* **distributing to each one individually as He wills."**
(1 Corinthians 12:4-11 NKJV)

The Gift of Faith

Faith can be given by the Holy Spirit as a gift. This gift is given to the individual as a gift to the Church. I became a Christian in 1982, and since then, the Lord has used me many times with the gift of faith. What seems to happen with the gift of faith is that when you pray for something, which would normally be unusually hard to believe, but you simply believe it will happen.

I will give you some examples of the prayers of faith the Lord has used me to pray.

I asked the Lord to provide a friend of mine with a violin. I asked first for a very good one. Then I went back to prayer and asked for a Stradivarius. I then went back and asked for a Stradivarius that was made in Stradivarius's best year. I then went back and asked that the Lord would release to her the best Stradivarius that was made during his best year.

Within a week she told me that she had been given a Stradivarius that was made in his best year. It is priceless!

Having some friends over for dinner, I had no food except for a frozen chicken. It was as hard as a table. I asked the Lord to defrost it. Laying my hands on it, the Lord defrosted it. We saw the water drip off the chicken and it was able to be cooked. This was before the invention of microwave ovens!

Multiplying Fish

When I was a student, I had very little money. One day as I was walking home with three little fishes, I asked that the Lord to multiply the fish for me, so that I could invite friends over for meals during the weekend. On arriving home, there were still only three fishes.

I refused to get despondent over this, so I rang my first friend Chris to invite him over for a meal. When he arrived, I discovered that he brought a box of fish with him; he was a chef and he brought it from work. Another friend who was also called Chris said to me that he had left fish in the refrigerator for me. I now had a fridge full of fish on each level, and I was able to invite friends over for the weekend meals.

Buying A Shop With No Money
I obtained my first shop when I had no money. I purchased it with faith. After praying for the shop, the Lord said to me that He would give it to me. I asked Him how He would do this. He said, "Do everything you can, and I will do the rest." I ended up with a three-story building, which I bought in 1989.

Arriving On Time
I was late for a particular prayer meeting. Sitting on a tube train, I wondered how I could speed up the process. I thought that I would pray specifically that when I arrived at the next tube station that my train would stop next to a platform that would have a train waiting to take me to Earl's Court. When I arrived at the next station, the train stopped next to another platform, where there was a train waiting. I jumped on the train, sat down, and asked another passenger whether the train was going to Earl's Court. "No," he said, and he explained that it was going somewhere else.

"Lord," I exclaimed, "I prayed that it would go there."

Just then the operator suddenly announced, "Would everyone on the train at platform five get off; it is now going to Earl's Court." Praise the Lord, I was not late for the prayer meeting.

Various Healings
I have prayed for a lady who was going blind, and she was instantly healed. Another case involved a man in a hospital, who had a lump the size of an orange that needed to be removed from his lungs. I prayed for him, and the lump completely disappeared. They had to cancel his operation!

I've seen healings come to people afflicted with arthritis, damaged legs, twisted spines, heart conditions, blood problems, and all manner of sickness and disease.

Faith also comes simply by spending time with Jesus, talking to the Holy Spirit, allowing His presence to come upon you, listening to Him, and being His friend.

When you spend time with someone, you become like them. When you allow the Holy Spirit to dwell within you, His character starts to bear fruit in your life. These elements of His character are described in Scripture as "the fruit of the spirit."

> 22"But the fruit of the Spirit is love, joy, peace, longsuffering, gentleness, goodness, _____,
> 23 meekness, temperance: against such there is no law."
> **(Galatians 5:22-23 KJV)**

Another way to receive faith is to hear God speak. This is incredibly important, and it is an effective way of growing in faith.

> "So then _____ _____ _____ _____, and hearing by the word of God."
> **(Romans 10:17 NKJV)**

10. How does faith come?_____

I was praying one day and the Lord said to me, "Martin, do you know there is an animal that uses faith?" After a little guessing, I asked him which one it was. He told me that it was the bat.

A bat has very poor vision, so to substantiate what he cannot see, he emits a sound; the sound bounces off the objects around him, and he hears the sound coming back to him. Thus, he is able to know what he cannot see. It is a little like radar.

If we examine this process, then we can see how *Hebrews11:1* and *Romans 10:17* work together. Also, we can learn from the bat how to walk/fly in faith.

> "Now faith is the substance of things hoped for, the evidence of things not seen."
> **(Hebrews 11:1 NKJV)**

> "So then **faith comes by hearing**, and hearing by the word of God."
> **(Romans 10:17 NKJV)**

The bat substantiates what he cannot see by hearing.

I think there is a lot more than this to understand from *Romans 10:17*, however.

When you are praying for something in faith, you need to emit a signal. That signal is talking to God. When you hear the response from God, you gain faith, and this substantiates the request. Because you are hearing His response to your prayer, you are asking for His opinion, and when He gives it, it encourages you and you believe what you have heard. Faith is being transmitted to you by the responses. Thus, faith comes by hearing, and hearing by the Word of God.

Often the mistake is to pray without hearing; then, when time goes by and nothing seems to be happening, doubts can creep in. Rather, we should keep talking to God and then listen to His replies about the situation in order to gain strength through His words and receive the faith that is transmitted with His words, thereby substantiating the unseen.

The next way we can receive faith is found in the Book of Jude:

> *"But you, beloved, building yourselves up on your most holy faith,*
> _____ _____ _____ _____ _____"*
> ***(Jude 1:20 NKJV)***

11. How do we build up our faith? _____

It is possible to build your faith simply by praying in the Holy Spirit, praying in tongues.

Have you ever asked someone to pray for you, and they've said a few words, and yet you feel nothing has really happened?

In such a case, we must rely on the truth of God's Word:

> *16b "The _____, _____ _____ of a righteous man avails much. 17 Elijah was a man with a nature like ours, and he prayed earnestly that it would not rain; and it did not rain on the land for three years and six months.*
> *18 And he prayed again, and the heaven gave rain, and the earth produced its fruit"*
> ***(James 5:16b-18 NKJV)***

Also, Jesus would sometimes pray and heal people with very few words:

> *5 "Now when Jesus had entered Capernaum, a centurion came to Him, pleading with Him,*
> *6 saying, "Lord, my servant is lying at home paralyzed, dreadfully tormented."*
> *7 And Jesus said to him, "I will come and heal him."*
> *8 The centurion answered and said, "Lord, I am not worthy that You should come under my roof. But only speak a word, and my servant will be healed....*
> *13 Then Jesus said to the centurion, "Go your way; and as*

you have believed, so let it be done for you." And his servant was healed
that same hour."
(Matthew 8:5-13 NKJV)

12. What did Jesus say to heal the centurion's servant? _____
_____

The answer is that few words need to be said when you have the necessary faith. Yet so much prayer is given without faith. In such cases the prayer may be sprinkled with a little hope, but not faith.

This where the verse from Jude that I alluded to earlier can help us. We need to build our faith by praying in the Holy Spirit.

Let me give you an example. A friend of mine told me that his wife had been separated from him, he was living in London, and that she had been placed in a psychiatric hospital in the United States.

This separation had lasted for some time; I believe it lasted at least eighteen months. I felt very angry about this when I realized that his wife could be taken from him with an ocean separating them. I asked him whether anyone had prayed about it. He told me that many had prayed. But on hearing this, in the center of my being, I did not believe that real effective prayer had taken place. I sensed that it had been only empty prayer.

I determined that I was going to pray about it. I realized that to pray effectively, I would need to have a mechanism in place to keep my praying focused until the goal was achieved. Therefore, I started by asking God to give me a burden for the needs. I then started praying in tongues and pushing against the burden I had been given. I prayed for what seemed like the whole night. The next night I slept in the lounge, so that I could pray loudly without disturbing anyone. Again I prayed for what seemed like the whole night. The third night I had been praying for about an hour or so when suddenly the burden lifted. There was no more reason to pray; I now *knew* the prayer had been answered, for I felt "light" in my spirit and I wanted to praise God. I truly knew the prayer had been answered.

Within a couple of weeks, this lady had been healed, and she was back with her husband in London.

Let's take a look now at the mechanics of this prayer. When I started the session of prayer, I did not know that the prayer had been answered. If I had known the prayer was answered, there would have been no need to continue in prayer. After many hours of prayer I suddenly *knew* the prayer was answered. Something had changed; *knowing* that the prayer was answered had given me great faith. So I had *built* myself up in faith by praying in the Holy Spirit.

This progression of prayer can also be found in Philippians:

> *6 "Be anxious for nothing, but in everything by _____ and*
> *_____, with _____, let your*
> *requests be made known to God;*
> *7 and the peace of God, which surpasses all understanding, will guard*
> *your hearts and minds through Christ Jesus."*
> ***(Philippians 4:6-7 NKJV)***

First Stage: We Start Praying.

Second Stage: Make Supplications.

As we pray, we begin to include our supplications. Just as you can reason with your earthly father for a request, we can reason with God as to why we want Him to honor our requests. I chose to do this stage of prayer in tongues, but it can be done in your own natural language, as well. The important thing is not to go to stage three before you know the prayer has been answered. Sometimes people will suggest that you go to stage three prematurely; they will state that by thanking God you are displaying your faith.

I disagree with this because it is important for your development in prayer to ***know*** you have the faith. Hope alone does not make prayer work. Thanking God for the answer to a prayer when you don't yet really believe that the answer is given is premature. You don't want a premature baby, because it might die, and you don't want to prematurely thank God for what you do not yet believe, because you don't want the prayer to die.

To thank God prematurely is not appropriate, because not enough has been accomplished to enable you to achieve the desired result. Continue in prayer until your spirit bursts with joy, ***knowing*** the prayer is answered. If you do not know the prayer has been answered, you do not yet have the faith for the prayer to be answered.

We can ask God for more faith, and we can ask Him to help us in our unbelief. *(See Mark 9:24.)*

I was once locked out of my house. Knowing that a builder who had a set of keys had been working there, I prayed that the Lord would send him around the corner immediately so I could get in with his key. I had left my clarinets in the house, and it was getting close to the time when I would be late for a rehearsal.

The Lord asked me, "Do you believe I will send him?"

I answered, "I half believe."

The Lord responded to me by saying, "I can't half send him."

What fun it is working for God. I responded to the Lord that although I only half believed He could send him, I did believe He could get me into the house. Within a minute, I was in the house.

Remember, if you only half believe, God can't "half do."

Third Stage: Giving of Thanks.

Fourth Stage: Receiving of Peace.

It seems to me that when God gives us peace after a session of prayer, our receiving of peace is God's "calling card" that the prayer request is now in His hands and has been answered.

Let us not take this process of prayer in vain, rushing through the stages without truly being respectful of the process. Failing in prayer does not encourage us or those we are praying for.

The effective, fervent prayer of the righteous man achieves much. *(See James 5:16.)*

Much prayer is done from a sincere heart, but sincerity alone does not bring the answer to prayer. We need effective, sincere prayer. Empty prayer, prayer that is devoid of faith, is not effective. We should not kid ourselves when we are praying for ourselves and other people by saying that we have faith when we don't really have faith. This causes disappointment, and it breeds unbelief.

If you go into a BMW store and try to buy a new car but don't have enough money, you will only embarrass yourself and the salesman. In that case you will go away disappointed. If you try to give £10 for a £50,000 car, it will not be accepted simply because you don't have enough money to pay for the automobile. Don't get upset by this, for this is reality. If you do not have enough authority or money, then you will be unable to purchase the vehicle. However, you can go away and try to increase the amount of money you have to enable you to buy the car.

Likewise, if you do not have the faith to "purchase" a prayer request, you will have to go and find the faith you need. You can build up your faith by praying in the Holy Spirit.

> 5 *"Now the end of the commandment is charity out of a pure heart, and of a good conscience, and of faith _____:*
> 6 *From which some having swerved have turned aside unto vain jangling."*
> **(1 Timothy 1:5-6 KJV)**

When we have feigned faith, it is vain jangling.

Notes

God Wanted to Speak

I have another interesting example to share with you.

Around 1985 I was in a fast-food restaurant in Earl's Court in London. As I was eating my food, I became aware that the Lord wanted me to talk to one of the servers about Him.

By the time I had mustered the courage to get up and speak to him, he had disappeared into one of the back rooms. I asked the manager if he could get him so that I could speak to him. The manager asked me, "Why?"

I was a little embarrassed by his question, so I said, "Because God wants me to speak to him."

At that point, the whole restaurant went quiet, or so it seemed. The manager brought the man out to me. I talked to him and found out that his name was Sunday. He wondered why God would want me to help him. He told me that he came from Ghana, and before he left for London, he had met a girl whom he had only spoken to for about a day. He felt God wanted him to marry this young lady. As it was very difficult for some to get visas to come to England, he was unsure with regard to how he should progress with his desires. I simply prayed in one or two sentences that God would bring the girl over from Ghana and be married to him.

About one month later she agreed to marry him, got a visa, crossed the ocean, and married him! I was honored to be a guest at their wedding.

Do you see how I did not have to spend days praying in tongues with regard to this prayer? My earlier intercession for my friend's wife to be reunited with her husband from across the ocean, had given me the faith to be able to pray simply, without intercession, for this lady to cross the ocean.

The Motives of Our Hearts

The next way of obtaining faith is the most important one of all. It involves the motives of our hearts.

5 "And the apostles said to the Lord, '_____ _____
_____.'

6 So the Lord said, 'If you have faith as a mustard seed, you can say to this mulberry tree, "Be pulled up by the roots and be planted in the sea," and it would obey you.
7 And which of you, having a servant plowing or tending sheep, will say to him when he has come in from the field, 'Come at once and sit down to eat'?

8 But will he not rather say to him, 'Prepare something for my supper, and gird yourself and serve me till I have eaten and drunk, and afterward you will eat and drink'?
9 Does he thank that servant because he did the things that were commanded him? I think not.
*10 So likewise you, when you have done all those things which you are commanded, say, '**We are unprofitable servants.** We have done what was our duty to do.'"*
(Luke 17:5-10 NKJV)

The apostles wanted the Lord to increase their faith, but what was the point the Lord was making to them? I think the answer can be found in verse 10: "When you have done all those things which you are commanded, say, 'We are unprofitable servants.'"

I think the translation here is a little awkward. This may be deliberate on God's part; perhaps He wants us to dig to find a nugget.

If we look in *Strong's Dictionary* for the definition of the word that is translated as "unprofitable," we find this:

Strong's Reference No. 888 ἀχρεῖος achreios
Meaning: 1) useless, good for nothing
Usage: AV - unprofitable

Therefore, this word could be translated as "When you have done all those things which you are commanded, say, 'We are useless servants!'"

However, this doesn't quite get to the heart of it, as it goes beyond self-deprecation. I am a useless servant. I am a good-for-nothing servant.

Yet it is possible to see clearly what Jesus was saying to the apostles:

No. 1—In response to their request to increase their faith, Jesus said that if they had faith as a mustard seed, they could . . . . Basically **when** you have the substance called faith, it will easily achieve the result, which is released through talking:

"Ye might say unto this sycamine tree, be thou plucked up by the root, and be thou planted in the sea; and it should obey you."
(Luke 17:6 KJV)

No. 2—Having the faith is NOT the important thing. What is important is your heart attitude. Do you want to work miracles? Why? Do you want everyone to look at you while you do the miracles? Do you want to receive the praises of men when they see you do miracles?

God is not looking for showmen and magicians.

At this point, the apostles' motives were not quite right. They wanted the power, but not from completely pure motives.

Faith is energized through love. Our attitude with regard to working miracles should be the compulsion that comes from compassion for the sick, the needy, and the lost.

Jesus questioned the motives of the apostles. Our attitude should be one of a useless servant. But what I really think this means is that when we perform a miracle, we should make it clear that this great power that works through us exists because we are *servants* of God and that the *use* of God's power did not come from us. The power is not inherent in us from our own self-developed abilities. Rather, the *use* is not from us, the power is not from us; we are *useless* servants who are simply administering the gift of God for the recipients through obedience.

The first time I taught on this passage of Scripture the Lord backed up the preaching by instantly healing a man. He had been in a motorcycle accident many years before and could not walk properly. The Lord was gracious to him and instantly healed his legs as I prayed for him.

It is interesting to see how Peter would try to imitate Jesus in his faith. We can learn a great deal from this:

> 25b *"Jesus went unto them, walking on the sea.*
> 26 *And when the disciples saw him walking on the sea, they were troubled, saying, it is a spirit; and they cried out for fear.*
> 27 *But straightway Jesus spake unto them, saying, Be of good cheer; it is I; be not afraid.*
> 28 *And Peter answered him and said, Lord, if it be thou, bid me come unto thee on the water.*
> 29 *And he said, Come. And when Peter was come down out of the ship,* **he walked on the water**, *to go to Jesus.*
> 30 *But when he saw the wind boisterous, he was afraid; and* **beginning to sink**, *he cried, saying, Lord, save me.*
> 31 *And immediately Jesus stretched forth his hand, and caught him, and said unto him, _____ _____ _____ _____ _____,*
> **wherefore didst thou   doubt?"**
> *(Matthew 14:25b-31KJV)*

As I have mentioned previously, faith is like money. Too often we waver in our faith, using the will of God as an excuse for our failures. The above portion of Scripture is interesting because it shows us that the will of God remains a constant, while the effect of Peter's faith shows contrasting results.

We can see that Jesus asked Peter to come to Him on the water. Now I am fairly sure Jesus did not then change His mind and decide He would like Peter to start sinking! So, what was the difference between success and failure? Jesus gives us the answer to this question: ***"O thou of little faith, wherefore didst thou doubt?"***

Peter's faith was small, and it was overridden by his doubts. The doubts were caused by his eyes looking at the boisterous wind and then coming to the conclusion that he would no longer be able to walk on the water.

The enemy of faith is unbelief. Unbelief is caused by doubts, anxieties, and fear.

Fading Faith

In my life I have noticed different levels of faith at different times. Like many, the honeymoon period when you first get saved is a time of great faith. Having now been able to see the Kingdom of Heaven, it is such a great surprise when all one's friends don't immediately get saved when you tell them the truth about the Kingdom. The important thing to remember, of course, is that the individual must have faith, not necessarily his or her friends.

I would pray for unusual things because God gave me a gift of faith. Having been taught that one should step out in faith, I would look for an action for my faith. For example, if I were late for a class at the Royal Academy of Music, I would pray that I would be able to run to the end of the road and jump and that I would land on a bus that would take me to college. Not being able to see around the corner, and not knowing the bus routes, I would set off and jump. I indeed landed on the back of a bus, the route-master busses that you have in London, which have an open, small platform on the back, which was traveling to a stop right outside my college. What laughter I would have when this would happen.

One night I was traveling on a bus that was coming back from the north of England. I really wanted a cup of coffee, but it was 1:30 in the morning. Again, in looking for an action, I asked God if He would put a cup of coffee into my hand if I closed my eyes and stuck my hand up into the air in the shape of a cup. As I closed my eyes and raised my hand, somebody put a cup of coffee into my hand. The only problem was that it did not contain sugar. Maybe I should have asked for that, as well!

The difficulty, though, is that faith, like coffee can go cold. After a while the number of miracles I saw began to fade. It was as if it would have been hard for me to pray for my coffee to be warm right after I had made it.

Why did my faith fade?

When Peter first started walking on the water, he was looking at Jesus; he started to sink when he started looking at the effects of the boisterous wind instead of looking at Jesus.

Often we can spend too much time looking at television or other attractions. If we look at those things too much or look at the wrong things, our faith will deteriorate.

Our relationship with Jesus changes as we get older. The effervescence of the honeymoon love we once had for Him changes to a stronger, trusting love that emanates from the adversities of life.

It was important for me to understand that my level of faith had been given to me as a gift. For me to understand people with different gifts and talents, I needed to see my life as a Christian without that faith. That type of faith was removed but then given back to me in a different way. I can say that my faith has gone through a maturing process with less frivolity, but it still leads me to pray for some unusually hard things.

For example, the Lord has said that He will give me a six-billion-pound skyscraper. I have had this confirmed from some other ministers, and I fully believe it will happen. He has told me that it will be used to "beam the gospel into every nation on the earth."

I think that middle-aged Christians can often fade in their faith towards God and sink into mediocrity. We need to take Paul's words to heart and press towards the high calling of God.

> 13b *"This one thing I do, forgetting those things which are behind, and reaching forth unto those things which are before, ...*
> 14 I _____ _____ _____ _____ *for the prize of the high calling of God in Christ Jesus."*
> **(Philippians 3:13b-14 NKJV)**

Counterfeit Faith

In addition to unbelief, fear, doubts, anxieties, and fretting, another enemy of faith is what I call counterfeit faith.

This is a serious problem because it causes even good Christians to stop praying. They pray with counterfeit faith, and nothing happens. Their prayer is not answered, and they lose hope and stop praying.

I have on a number of occasions gone to the bank to deposit the business receipts only to find that a £20 note is a counterfeit. In such a case the note is taken from me, and then it is sent to the Bank of England. What I thought was genuine was in fact worthless. It looked correct and felt correct, but it did not carry the authority of the Bank of England; therefore, it is a worthless piece of paper.

Sometimes we pray and we genuinely believe that we are going to get the answer to the prayer and yet it doesn't happen. Why? Because it is *counterfeit* faith!

I think some of the confusion stems from the translation of words in the New Testament Greek into English.

> 21 "Jesus answered and said unto them, Verily I say unto you, If ye have _____, and doubt not, ye shall not only do this which is done to the fig tree, but also if ye shall say unto this mountain, Be thou removed, and be thou cast into the sea; it shall be done.
> 22 And all things, whatsoever ye shall ask in prayer, _____, ye shall receive."
> **(Matthew 21:21-22 KJV)**

Matthew 21:21 says, "If you have faith," yet in *verse 22* it says, "believing ye shall receive."

Both the words that are translated as "faith" (4102) and "believing" (4100) come from the same root word in Greek. *Strong's Dictionary* provides us with the following definitions:

Strong's Reference No. 4102   πίστις   pistis
Meaning:
conviction of the truth of anything, belief; in the NT of a conviction or belief respecting man's relationship to God and divine things, generally with the included idea of trust and holy fervor born of faith and joined with it
 1a) relating to God
 1a1) the conviction that God exists and is the creator and ruler of all things, the provider and bestower of eternal salvation through Christ
 1b) relating to Christ
 1b1) a strong and welcome conviction or belief that Jesus is the Messiah, through whom we obtain eternal salvation in the kingdom of God
 1c) the religious beliefs of Christians
 1d) belief with the predominate idea of trust (or confidence) whether in God or in Christ, springing from faith in the same 2) fidelity, faithfulness
 2a) the character of one who can be relied on

Strong's Reference No. 4100 πιστεύω pisteuo
Meaning:
1) to think to be true, to be persuaded of, to credit, place confidence in 1a) of the thing believed
2) 1a1) to credit, have confidence 1b) in a moral or religious reference
3) 1b1) used in the NT of the conviction and trust to which a man is impelled by a certain inner and higher prerogative and law of soul 1b2) to trust in Jesus or God as able to aid either in obtaining or in doing something: saving faith
4) 1bc) mere acknowledgment of some fact or event: intellectual faith 2) to entrust a thing to one, i.e. his fidelity 2a) to be entrusted with a thing

The reason why this is so important is that in English the word "believe" doesn't have the same strength as the word "faith."

The issue is not whether you believe something, for that doesn't mean you have faith. For example, a few hundred years ago scientists believed that the world was flat. Just because they believed it, did not make it true. Many scientists now believe we come from monkeys, but that does not make it true.

> *"And all things, whatsoever ye shall ask in prayer, **believing**, ye shall receive."*
> *(Matthew 21:22 KJV)*

Really this verse should say: "And all things, whatsoever ye shall ask in prayer, *in faith*, ye shall receive."

Solely having belief does not mean you have faith. It may almost look the same as faith, just as counterfeit money looks the same as real money, but there is a difference.

Real faith is a substance; it is the evidence of things not seen. This is a quality of belief that is backed up by genuine evidence and authority.

> *"Now the end of the commandment is charity out of a pure heart, and of a good conscience, and of **faith unfeigned**."*
> *(1 Timothy 1:5 KJV)*

> *"Now faith is the substance of things hoped for, the evidence of things not seen."*
> *(Hebrews 11:1 KJV)*

How can we tell the difference between faith and belief?

Admittedly, this is difficult in the same way it is difficult to see the difference between genuine and counterfeit currency.

The main difference I would look for focuses on where you are believing?

> *"For _____ _____ _____ man believeth (**pisteuo**, faith) unto righteousness."*
> *(Romans 10:10 KJV)*

13. What do we believe with?_____
Do you have a real belief in the center of your being that is backed up with joy over the fact that your prayer has been answered? If you don't have the joy, then maybe the faith is just belief or hope.

Conversely, I have found that there can be a battle in the mind when you are praying in faith. This can confuse the person who is praying by leading them to think that he or she doesn't have faith and is wavering. In this situation the mind is a battlefield. Sometimes when I am praying in faith for something, in my mind I hear Satan saying, "God won't do that for you; God won't do that for you." When this happens, the devil is trying to corrupt my faith. Once the prayer has been answered, however, he usually changes his tune to: "God didn't do it, God didn't do it." I don't think his tactics have changed much through the centuries.

When you want to distinguish between faith and belief, keep talking to God. Listening to His replies will help you establish what real faith is. On many occasions I have received wonderful presents from God simply by being patient and listening to what He has to say. Sometimes He will say to me, "Wait," or "Not yet." Each time I have waited, however, I have received something much better.

***Without doubt,
listening to God is the best way to receive faith.***

Reflections
1. What is faith?
2. How does faith come?
3. What animal uses faith?
4. What type of money is faith?
5. How do you increase your faith?

Applications
Cultivate a habit of making sure that everything you say, comes to pass.
Study the heroes of faith in *Hebrews Chapter 11*.

Memory Verses
"Now faith is the substance of things hoped for, the evidence of things not seen."
(Hebrews 11:1 KJV)

"But without faith it is impossible to please him: for he that cometh to God must believe that he is, and that he is a rewarder of them that diligently seek him."
(Hebrews 11:6 KJV)

"So then faith cometh by hearing, and hearing by the word of God."
(Romans 10:17 KJV)

"For by grace are ye saved through faith; and that not of yourselves: it is the gift of God:"
(Ephesians 2:8 KJV)

Closing Prayer

O Father, forgive me for neglecting the enormous importance of growing in faith. Your world so needs effectual prayer, energized by faith. Please release to me the faith that will please Jesus, so that He will not be disappointed when he returns to Earth. I ask this in the name of Jesus. Amen.

Patience
Chapter Thirteen – Study Guide

Opening Prayer
    Dear Father, help me to appreciate patience, it's fruit, and your perfect timings. I ask this in the name of Jesus. Amen.

The following questions will be answered during study of this chapter:
1. What is the fruit of patience?
2. Why should we pursue patience?
3. How do we obtain patience?
4. What is the most important part of a race?

Pursuit of Patience

"But you, O man of God, flee these things and pursue righteousness, godliness, faith, love, patience, gentleness."
(1 Timothy 6:11 NKJV)

Why have we been asked to pursue patience? What is so important about waiting? The Bible gives us a clear answer to these questions:

"My brethren, count it all joy when you fall into various trials, knowing that _____ _____ _____ _____ _____ _____ _____. But let patience have its perfect work, that you may be _____ and _____, lacking _____."
(James 1:2 NKJV)

1. What does the perfect work of faith do for us? _____
_____

2. What produces patience in us? _____

3. Why should we count it all joy when we fall into trials? _____
_____

Would you like to be perfect? Would you like to be complete? Would you like to lack nothing?

What a promise this is. The fruit of patience is perfection, wholeness, and lacking nothing!

> *"But that on the good ground are they, which in an honest and good heart, having heard the word, keep it, and bring forth fruit with patience."*
> *(Luke 8:15 KJV)*

4. What does patience bring forth? _____

> *"In your patience possess ye your souls."*
> *(Luke 21:19 KJV)*

5. What can we possess with patience? _____

> *"To them who by patient continuance in well doing seek for glory and honour and immortality, eternal life:"*
> *(Romans 2:7 KJV)*

6. What can we seek for with patience? _____

> *12 "That ye be not slothful, but followers of them who through faith and patience _____ _____ _____.*
> *13 For when God made promise to Abraham, because he could swear by no greater, he sware by himself,*
> *14 Saying, Surely blessing I will bless thee, and multiplying I will multiply thee.*
> *15 And so, after he had patiently endured, he obtained the promise."*
> *(Hebrews 6:12-15 KJV)*

7. What else do we receive from patience? _____

> *"Remembering without ceasing your work of faith, and labour of love, and _____ of hope in our Lord Jesus Christ, in the sight of God and our Father;"*
> *(1 Thessalonians 1:3 KJV)*

8. How is hope expressed? _____

When we hope, we are expectant. As we learn to hope, then we eagerly wait for the answer of our hope.

> *24 "For we are saved by hope: but hope that is seen is not hope: for what a man seeth, why doth he yet hope for?*
> *25 But if we hope for that we see not, then do we _____ _____ _____ for it."*
> *(Romans 8:24-25 KJV)*

Now let us read *Romans 5:1-5* very carefully because it shows us how we receive patience.

> *3b ...we glory in tribulations also: knowing that tribulation worketh*
> _____*;*
> *4 And patience, experience; and experience, hope:*
> *5 And hope maketh not ashamed; because the love of God is shed abroad in our hearts by the Holy Ghost which is given unto us."*
> **(Romans 5:3b-5 KJV)**

When we are experiencing tribulation, we have no choice but to weather it. To our souls it is comparable to a sword being heated in the fire in an effort to strengthen it. Each time we have to go through a tribulation we find it easier to endure, because we have experienced tribulation before. Each time we go through tribulation God brings us safely through, so why should we worry about the next tribulation we have to face?

In this way we are learning to be patient, to wait under pressure, knowing God will come through on our behalf. The more experience we have of God coming through for us, the more expectation we will have of Him. In this way we find hope. Hope is like a torch in a dark tunnel. It tells us that we will get through, that things will change.

Now we can see why James says to count it all joy when we encounter various trials. The testing we go through produces patience in our lives. Once we have patience, praying for things becomes easier, because we will be happy to wait for God to answer the prayers. As we mature in faith and patience we will no longer doubt every few minutes if we don't see the answer we want.

Pay attention to Solomon's wise words:

> *"The* _____ _____ _____ _____ *is better than its*
> *beginning, and* _____ *is better than pride"*
> **(Ecclesiastes 7:8 NIV)**

Never forget that the end of a matter is more important than the beginning!!!!!!!

Reflections
1. What is the fruit of patience?
2. Why should we pursue it?
3. How do we obtain patience?
4. What is the most important part of a race?

Memory Verses

"But you, O man of God, flee these things and pursue righteousness, godliness, faith, love, patience, gentleness."
(1 Timothy 6:11 NKJV)

"The end of a matter is better than its beginning, and patience is better than pride."
(Ecclesiastes 7:8 NIV)

2 "My brethren, count it all joy when you fall into various trials,
3 knowing that the testing of your faith produces patience,
4 But let patience have its perfect work, that you may be perfect and complete, lacking nothing"
(James 1:2-4 NKJV)

Closing Prayer

Dear Father, please help me to work with patience and not haste. Help me to be like a master musician that pays attention to the end of a phrase. Give me a rhythm that will give me the endurance to win my race. I ask for these in the name of Jesus. Amen.

God's Provision
Chapter Fourteen – Study Guide

Opening Prayer
Dear Father, fill us with the wonderful knowledge of your provision for Your children. Let us not lean on our own understanding, but establish our trust on Your love and Your Word. I ask this in the name of Jesus. Amen.

The following questions will be answered during study of this chapter:
1. Who is worthy of his wages?
2. What do the Gentiles seek after?
3. What is our first priority?

Sowing and Reaping

There are many people who do not have jobs. The following commandment is not for those who cannot find work, but it is for those who don't want to work.

> *"For even when we were with you, we commanded you this: If anyone _____ _____ _____, neither shall he eat."*
> **(2 Thessalonians 3:10 NKJV)**

In *our* walk with God we should always be working for Him. There are many things we can be doing:

1. Working in full-time ministry.
2. Working in jobs so as to produce finances and being the salt of the world.
3. Helping the church, helping the Pastor, etc.
4. Special ministries for the Lord, such as intercession (prayer), evangelism, etc.

Our lives should consist of a combination of the above. Notice what Jesus has to say about this: To sum up this "work" that we do, can be found in *Matthew 6:33.*

25 "Therefore I say unto you, Take no thought for your life, what ye shall eat, or what ye shall drink; nor yet for your body, what ye shall put on. Is not the life more than meat, and the body than raiment?

26 Behold the fowls of the air: for they sow not, neither do they reap, nor gather into barns; yet your heavenly Father --- _____ _____. Are ye not much better than they?

27 Which of you by _____ _____ can add one cubit unto his stature?

28 And why take ye thought for raiment? Consider the lilies of the field, how they grow; they toil not, neither do they spin:

29 And yet I say unto you, That even Solomon in all his glory was not arrayed like one of these.

30 Wherefore, if God so clothe the grass of the field, which today is, and tomorrow is cast into the oven, shall he not much more clothe you, O ye of little faith?

31 Therefore take no thought, saying, What shall we eat? or, What shall we drink? or, Wherewithal shall we be clothed?

32 (For after all these things do the Gentiles seek) for your heavenly Father _____ _____ _____ _____ of all these things.

33 But seek ye** _____ **the kingdom of God, and his** _____; **and all these things** _____ _____ _____ **unto you.

34 Take therefore no thought for the morrow: for the morrow shall take thought for the things of itself. Sufficient unto the day is the evil thereof."
(Matthew 6:25-34 KJV)

1. What are the three things the Gentiles seek after?
   1. _____
   2. _____
   3. _____

2. Who feeds the fowls of the air? _____

3. What does Father know that we need? _____

4. Will He clothe us? _____

5. What stops us believing that? _____

6. We are not asked to seek that which the Gentiles strive for. What are we asked to seek for? _____

_____

7. When we have our priorities correct and seek first what Father asks us to, what does He do in response? _____

_____

We see from this passage that God will provide for us in every way, including basic physical necessities, **when we comply with His condition** of seeking first the Kingdom of God.

> 4 "Carry neither _____ _____, _____ , nor
> _____; and greet no one along the road.
> 5 But whatever house you enter, first say, 'Peace to this house.'
> 6 And if a son of peace is there, your peace will rest on it; if not, it will return to you.
> 7 And remain in the same house, eating and drinking such things as they give, for the labourer is _____ of his _____. Do not go from house to house."
> **(Luke 10:4-7 NKJV)**

8. Why did Jesus tell the disciples not to take a money bag with them?

_____

9. Who is worthy of his wages? _____

When Jesus sent His disciples out to work for Him, He told them to take no money with them and no bags for food or extra shoes. It wasn't because He wanted them to be poor, but that they would know that when they were working for Him He would provide for everything. When you work for God, God pays!!

Notice when Jesus sent them out He did not say they did not have any money, but not to *take* a money bag with them. They must have had money bags for Jesus to say not to take them.

Let us read how God provided for the children of Israel when they were in the wilderness.

> 14 "And when the layer of dew lifted, there, on the surface of the wilderness, was a _____ _____
> _____, as fine as frost on the ground.
> 15 So when the children of Israel saw it, they said to one another, "What is it?" For they did not know what it was. And Moses said to them, "This is the bread which the LORD has given you to eat.
> 16 "This is the thing which the LORD has commanded: 'Let every man gather it according to each one's need, one omer for each person, according to the number of persons; let every man take for those who are in his tent.'"

17 Then the children of Israel did so and gathered, some more, some less. So when they measured it by omers, he who gathered much had nothing left over, and he who gathered little had no lack. ...
31 And the house of Israel called its name _____. And it was like white coriander seed, and the taste of it was like wafers made with honey."
(Exodus 16:14-31 NKJV)

10. What is the name of the small round substance? _____

11. Did any have lack? _____

12. What about those who were only able to gather little, did they lack?

_____

13. Why did they not lack? _____

In writing the second letter to the Corinthians, Paul mentions this passage when he says that our abundance provides for others' lack, and their abundance provides for our lack.

12 "For if there is first a willing mind, it is accepted according to what one has, and not according to what he does not have.
13 For I do not mean that others should be eased and you burdened;
14 but by an equality, that now at this time _____ _____ may supply _____ _____, that their abundance also may supply your lack— that there may be equality.
15 As it is written, "He who gathered much had nothing left over, and he who gathered little had no lack."
(2 Corinthians 8:12-15 NKJV)

So we see that when God provides for us, it is not just for ourselves but for others also.

"Give, and it will be given to you: good measure, pressed down, shaken together, and running over will be put into your bosom. For with the same measure that you use, it will be measured back to you."
(Luke 6:38 NKJV)

The Bible says that when we give, it is like sowing a seed into the ground. When we sow a little, we get a little back; when we sow bountifully, we shall reap bountifully.

6 "But this I say: He who sows sparingly will also _____ _____, and he who sows bountifully will also reap
_____.

7 So let each one give as he purposes in his heart, not grudgingly or of necessity; for God loves a cheerful giver.
8 And God is able to make all grace abound toward you, that you, always having all sufficiency in all things, may have _____ _____ for _____ good work."
(2 Corinthians 9:6-8 NKJV)

God Loves a Cheerful Giver

"Bring _____ _____ _____ into the storehouse, That there may be _____ in My house, And try Me now in this," Says the LORD of hosts, "If I will not open for you the windows of heaven And _____ _____ _____ _____ such blessing that there will not be room enough to receive it."
(Malachi 3:10 NKJV)

14. How does God provide for the Church—its upkeep, wages for ministers and musicians, and other needs? _____

_____

"Will a man _____ God? Yet you have robbed Me! But you say, 'In what way have we robbed You?' In _____ _____ _____."
(Malachi 3:8 NKJV)

15. What causes a lack of provision for the Church? _____

"Bring all the tithes into the storehouse, That there may be food in My house, And try Me now in this," Says the LORD of hosts, "If I will not open for you the windows of heaven And pour out for you _____ _____ That there will not be room enough to receive it."
(Malachi 3:10 NKJV)

16. What does God promise to do when we tithe? _____

"Beloved, I _____ _____ _____ _____ that thou mayest prosper and be in health, even as thy soul prospereth."
(3 John 1:2 KJV)

17. What does God desire for us? _____

"Let them shout for joy, and be glad, that favour my righteous cause: yea, let them say continually, Let the LORD be magnified, which hath _____ in the prosperity of his servant."
(Psalm 35:27 KJV)

18. What does God experience when his servants prosper? _____

When we give, God is pleased with us. He wants us to be cheerful givers, and He wants us to prosper.

When we give, it is not according to how much we give, but according to our heart and our ability.

> *41 "And Jesus sat over against the treasury, and beheld how the people cast money into the treasury: and many that were rich cast in much.*
> *42 And there came a certain poor widow, and she threw in _____ _____, which make a farthing.*
> *43 And he called unto him his disciples, and saith unto them, Verily I say unto you, That this poor widow hath cast _____ _____, than all they which have cast into the treasury:*
> *44 For all they did cast in of their abundance; but she of her want did cast in all that she had, even all her living."*
> **(Mark 12:41-44 KJV)**

19. Who cast the most into the treasury? _____

_____

> *"Finally let us remember the exhortation that God gave to Abraham: "Saying, _____ _____ I will bless thee, and multiplying I will multiply thee."*
> **(Hebrews 6:14 KJV)**

20. Who is going to bless us? _____

21. Is that promise sure? _____

God wants us to be blessed, and He wants us to be prosperous, but not just for ourselves; we are to reach out to others and to the Church, as well.

Let us remember what God has given to us:

> *"For God so loved the world, that _____ _____ his only begotten Son, that whosoever believeth in him should not perish, but have everlasting life."*
> **(John 3:16 KJV)**

Reflections
1. Who is worthy of his wages?
2. What do the Gentiles seek after?
3. What is our first priority?

Applications

Make a list of your worries and cares and cast them on the Lord DAILY. (Do not neglect to do this as worries and anxieties have a corrosive effect on our lives.)

Memory Verses

33 *"**But seek ye first the kingdom of God, and his righteousness***; and all these things shall be added unto you."*
(Matthew 6:33 KJV)

34 *"Take therefore no thought for the morrow: for the morrow shall take thought for the things of itself. Sufficient unto the day is the evil thereof."*
(Matthew 6:34 KJV)

7 *"Casting all your care upon him; for he careth for you."*
(I Peter 5:7 KJV)

6 *"Be careful for nothing; but in every thing by prayer and supplication with thanksgiving let your requests be made known unto God.*
7 And the peace of God, which passeth all understanding, shall keep your hearts and minds through Christ Jesus."
(Philippians 4:6-7 KJV)

Closing Prayer:

Dear Father, how You love us. Your provision is always faithful. Forgive us our unbelief, the staining of our clothes of righteousness with the sins of worry and anxiety. Forgive us our neglect of casting our cares upon you. Thank you that you deem us more valuable than the birds and the flowers. Let us forge ahead with the priority of seeking first the Kingdom of God, not weighted down with cares. Give us Your mercy and grace. I ask this in the name of Jesus. Amen.

Poverty and Our Debt to the Poor
Chapter Fifteen – Study Guide

Opening Prayer

Dear Father, help me to understand poverty, that I may be able to help the poor. I ask this in the name of Jesus. Amen

---

The following questions will be answered during study of this chapter:
1. What is the main benefit of being poor?
2. What was the iniquity of Sodom to the poor?
3. Who is it that makes people poor?
4. What do the lips of the righteous achieve?

Benefits of Being Poor

One of the benefits of being poor is that it is easier to *enter* the Kingdom of God in that state.

> *"Then said Jesus unto his disciples, Verily I say unto you, That a _____ _____ shall _____ enter into the kingdom of heaven. And again I say unto you, It is easier for a camel to go through the eye of a needle, than for a rich man to enter into the kingdom of God."*
> *(Matthew 19:23-24 KJV)*

1. How hard is it for a rich man to enter the Kingdom of God?

_____

> *"For ye know the grace of our Lord Jesus Christ, that, though he was rich, yet for your sakes he became poor, that ye through his poverty might be rich."*
> *(2 Corinthians 8:9 KJV)*

2. Once we enter the Kingdom of God does Jesus still want us to have poverty? _____

> *"Beloved, I wish above all things that thou mayest _____ and be in health, even as thy soul prospereth."*
> *(3 John 1:2 KJV)*

3. What does God want to happen to us? _____

_____

> *"Behold, this was the iniquity of thy sister Sodom, pride, fullness of bread, and abundance of idleness was in her and in her daughters,* **neither did she strengthen the hand of the _____ and_____."**
> **(Ezekiel 16:49 KJV)**

4. What was the condition of Sodom?_____

_____

5. Being full of bread what iniquity did Sodom do? _____

_____

When God prospers us, we then have a responsibility toward the poor. It is not good enough just to pray for the poor; you must feed them, as well.

When God destroyed Sodom, many people think that He did so only because of their sexual immorality. God destroyed Sodom because of the people's pride; having a fullness of bread, **they would not strengthen the hand of the poor and needy.**

Our faith must communicate more than just words.

What is Poverty?

In Deuteronomy God is explaining to the children of Israel that they had a choice either to obey God and be blessed, or to disobey Him and be cursed.

> 45 *"Moreover all these curses shall come upon thee, and shall pursue thee, and overtake thee, till thou be destroyed; because thou hearkenedst not unto the voice of the LORD thy God, to keep his commandments and his statutes which he commanded thee....*
> 48 *Therefore shalt thou serve thine enemies which the LORD shall send against thee, in _____, and in _____, and in _____, and in _____ _____ _____ things:*
> **(Deuteronomy 28:45-48 KJV)**

6. In verse 48, what four different aspects of poverty are there?

    1. _____

    2. _____

    3. _____

    4._____

When we have a "want of ALL things," we find that even our neighbors don't want to know us.

People who have severe needs are not always attractive to other people, often because their neediness is generally very visible. The opposite is also true, that rich people will always have many friends. *(See Proverbs 14:20 & 19:4.)*

We know that poverty ultimately comes from God when we make the choice to disobey Him, but how else can we be responsible for it?

> *"The righteous eateth to the satisfying of his soul: but the belly of* _____ _____ *shall want."*
> ***(Proverbs 13:25 KJV)***

7. What is it that brings want? _____

> *"The LORD maketh poor, and maketh rich: he bringeth low, and lifteth up"*
> ***(1 Samuel 2:7 KJV)***

8. Who makes us rich or poor? _____

> *"The lips of the righteous feed many: but* _____ _____ *for* _____ *of wisdom."*
> ***(Proverbs 10:21 KJV)***

9 . What lack causes fools to die? _____

_____

> *"Poverty and shame shall be to him that refuseth instruction: but he that regardeth reproof shall be honoured."*
> ***(Proverbs 13:18 KJV)***

10. What happens to him that refuseth instruction? _____

_____

> *9 "How long wilt thou sleep, O sluggard? when wilt thou arise out of thy sleep?*
> *10 Yet a little sleep, a little slumber, a little folding of the hands to sleep:*
> *11 So shall thy poverty come as one that travelleth, and thy want as an armed man."*
> ***(Proverbs 6:9-11 KJV)***

11. What comes quickly when you are lazy? _____

"He that loveth pleasure shall be a _____ man: he that loveth wine and oil shall not be rich."
(Proverbs 21:17 KJV)

12. What will hedonism, the seeking of pleasure, bring you? _____
_____

"He that _____ to be rich hath an evil eye, and considereth not that poverty shall come upon him."
(Proverbs 28:22 KJV)

13. Why is it futile to try and rush into riches? _____
_____

"He that _____ his land shall have plenty of bread: but he that followeth after vain persons shall have poverty enough."
(Proverbs 28:19 KJV)

Make sure you diligently do your work; don't waste your time by following empty philosophers, or you will have poverty:

Cry out to God, fear Him, and trust Him, and He will deliver you.

6 "This poor man _____, and the LORD heard him, and _____ him out of all his troubles.
7 The angel of the LORD encampeth round about them that fear him, and delivereth them.
8 O taste and see that the LORD is good: blessed is the man that trusteth in him.
9 O fear the LORD, ye his saints: for _____ _____ _____ _____ to them that fear him.
10 The young lions do lack, and suffer hunger: but they that seek the LORD shall not want any good thing."
(Psalm 34:6-10 KJV)

14. Why did the Lord respond to the poor man? _____
_____

15. What will those that seek the LORD lack? _____
_____

It is God who sends both poverty and wealth; He humbles and He exalts. *(See 1 Samuel 2:7.)*

Even though God sends poverty as a means of correction, He still loves the poor and desires to help them. He maintains their rights. *(See Psalm 140:12)*

The poor and the mighty are to be treated the same.

> *1 "My brethren, have not the faith of our Lord Jesus Christ, the Lord of glory, with respect of persons.*
> *2 For if there come unto your assembly a man with a gold **ring**, in goodly apparel, and there come in also a poor man in vile raiment;*
> *3 And ye have _____ to him that weareth the gay clothing, and say unto him, Sit thou here in a good place; and say to the poor, Stand thou there, or sit here under my footstool:*
> *4 Are ye not then partial in yourselves, and are become judges of _____ _____ ?"*
> **(James 2:1-4 KJV)**

16. When we treat people differently according to their wealth what are we doing? _____

_____

> *"And **also I have** _____ **the rain from you…** yet have ye not returned unto me, saith the LORD."*
> **(Amos 4:7 KJV)**

17. Why did the LORD withhold rain from the people? _____

_____

> *14 "And when he had spent all, **there arose a** _____ _____ in that land; and he began to be in want.*
> *15 And he went and joined himself to a citizen of that country; and he sent him into his fields to feed swine.*
> *16 And he would fain have filled his belly with the husks that the swine did eat: and no man gave unto him.*
> *17 And when he came to himself, he said, How many hired servants of my father's have bread enough and to spare, and I perish with hunger!*
> *18 **I will arise and go to my father, and will say unto him, Father, I have sinned against heaven, and before thee."***
> **(Luke 15:14-18 KJV)**

18. What event caused the son to come to his senses and return to his father? _____

"The Spirit of the Lord is upon me, because he hath _____
____ to preach the gospel to the poor; he hath sent me to heal the
brokenhearted, to preach deliverance to the captives, and
recovering of sight to the blind, to set at liberty them that are
bruised."
(Luke 4:18 KJV)

19. What was given to Jesus to help Him preach the good news to the

poor? _____

_____

*"For ye know the grace of our Lord Jesus Christ, that, **though he was***
rich, yet for your sakes he became poor, that ye through his poverty
might be rich."
(2 Corinthians 8:9 KJV)

20. What did Jesus sacrifice, in order for us to be rich? _____

_____

21. What have we been commanded to do for the poor?

"_____ ***the poor** and fatherless: do justice to the afflicted*
and needy."
(Psalm 82:3 KJV)

"He that _____ _____ **upon the poor lendeth unto the**
LORD; *and that which he hath given will he pay him again."*
(Proverbs 19:17 KJV)

"And if thy brother be waxen poor, *and fallen in decay with thee; then*
thou shalt _____ _____*: yea, though he be a stranger, or a*
sojourner; that he may live with thee."
(Leviticus 25:35 KJV)

"He that oppresseth the poor reproacheth his Maker: but he that
honoureth him _____ _____ **on the poor."**
(Proverbs 14:31 KJV)

Through the Church God has provided for us, in that we should be
dependent on one another, as His children and brothers and sisters in
Christ.

"Whoso _____ _____ _____ *at the cry of the poor,*
he also shall cry himself, but shall not be heard."
(Proverbs 21:13 KJV)

*"He that giveth unto the poor shall not lack: **but he that** _____*
_____ _____ ***shall have many a curse.***
(Proverbs 28:27 KJV)

22. What happens to us when we ignore the poor? _____

_____

"He that hath a bountiful eye _____ _____ _____;
for he giveth of his bread to the poor."
   (Proverbs 22:9 KJV)

*"Then Jesus beholding him loved him, and said unto him, One thing thou
lackest: go thy way, sell whatsoever thou hast, and give to the poor, and
thou shalt have _____in heaven: and come, take up the
cross, and follow me."*
(Mark 10:21 KJV)

"Blessed is he that _____ *the poor: the LORD will deliver
him in time of trouble. The LORD will preserve him, and keep him alive;
and he shall be blessed upon the earth: and thou wilt not deliver him
unto the will of his enemies."*
(Psalm 41:1-2 KJV)

23. What happens to us when we help the poor? _____

_____

In addition to helping the poor, we should fast. Fasting not only helps us to
empathize with the poor, but it also brings us spiritual power to loose
bands of wickedness, undo heavy burdens, let the oppressed go free, and
break every yoke. *(See Isaiah 58:6-12.)*

**By obeying God's commands to us with regard to the poor, He will
surely bless us.**

---

*1 "Praise ye the LORD. Blessed is the man that feareth the LORD, that
delighteth greatly in his commandments.*
*2 His seed shall be mighty upon earth: the generation of the upright shall
be blessed.*
*3 Wealth and riches shall be in his house: and his righteousness
endureth for ever.*
*4 Unto the upright there ariseth light in the darkness: he is gracious,
and full of compassion, and righteous.*
*5 A good man showeth favour, and lendeth: he will guide his affairs with
discretion.*
*6 Surely he shall not be moved for ever: the righteous shall be in
everlasting remembrance.*

7 He shall not be afraid of evil tidings: his heart is fixed, trusting in the LORD.
8 His heart is established, he shall not be afraid, until he see his desire upon his enemies.
*9 **He hath dispersed, he hath given to the poor**; his righteousness endureth for ever; his horn shall be exalted with honour."*
(Psalm 112:1-9 KJV)

24. List the blessings we receive when delight in the commandments of the Lord and disperse to the poor.

1. _____
2. _____
3. _____
4. _____

Reflections

1. What is the main benefit of being poor?
2. What was the iniquity of Sodom to the poor?
3. Who is it that makes people poor?
4. What do the lips of the righteous achieve?

Applications

Open your eyes to the poor around you and ask the Lord what to do for them.

Memory Verses

"For ye know the grace of our Lord Jesus Christ, that, though he was rich, yet for your sakes he became poor, that ye through his poverty might be rich."
(2 Corinthians 8:9 KJV)

*"**He that hath pity upon the poor lendeth unto the LORD;** and that which he hath given will he pay him again*
(Proverbs 19:17 KJV)

"The Lord maketh poor, and maketh rich: he bringeth low, and lifteth up."
(1 Samuel 2:7 KJV)

Closing Prayer

Dear Father, I understand that poverty is a curse, and that Jesus became poor so that we could be rich. Please help me to have an open heart to those in need, to be able to give and teach those who are in lack. I ask for this in the name of Jesus. Amen.

Borrowing, Debts, and How to Get Out of Debt
Chapter Sixteen – Study Guide

Opening Prayer
Dear Father, debt is such an acidic and debilitating condition. Please give me wisdom to help those who are in debt. I ask this in the name of Jesus. Amen.

The following questions will be answered during study of this chapter:
1. Are we allowed to borrow?
2. How do we receive financial curses?
3. How do we get out of debt?

Permission to Borrow

"Owe no man any thing, but to love one another: for he that loveth another hath fulfilled the law."
(Romans 13:8 KJV)

One might think that this verse teaches us that one is not allowed to borrow. In the light of the Scriptures below, however, we can see that God does at times allow us to borrow.

> *"If there be among you a poor man of one of thy brethren within any of thy gates in thy land which the LORD thy God giveth thee, thou shalt not harden thine heart, nor shut thine hand from thy poor brother: But thou shalt open thine hand wide unto him, and shalt _____ _____ _____ sufficient for his need, in that which he wanteth."*
> *(Deuteronomy 15:6-8 KJV)*

1. What does God ask us to do for the poor brother? _____
_____

2. Would God ask us to lend to our brothers if borrowing was wrong?
_____

3. Why, then, does *Romans 13:8* say that we should owe no man anything? _____

It seems to me that it means we should not withhold what we contract to do. For example, if we have a mortgage, we should keep up with the payments. If we have borrowed money from somebody, we should pay them back in the manner we agreed to.

When we don't pay back what we owe, we often receive curses in our lives.

Sowing and Reaping

These curses can prevent us from getting on with our lives. We can be working hard, yet never have enough to pay our bills. We can be tithing and giving our offerings, yet we find we still do not have enough. If this is the case in your life, you need to ask, "Is there a curse operating in my life?" If so, it is time to do some weeding. *(See Chapter 17.)*

> *"Give, and it shall be given unto you; good measure, pressed down, and shaken together, and running over, shall men give into your bosom. For with the same measure that ye mete withal it shall be measured to you again"*
> *(Luke 6:38 KJV).*

4. When we give, what is it that we receive back? _____

5. When a farmer sows wheat, what does he receive back? _____

_____

The farmer does not receive barley when he sows wheat.

6. What do you think we receive back when we give someone a curse?
E.g. borrowing, but not returning their property. _____

_____

Normally we look at the verse *Luke 6:38* with regard to giving someone something positive. But if you have given a person negative money, by borrowing from them and not paying it back, then the same will be given back to you. You will reap "negative money," good measure, pressed down, shaken together, and running over.

In other words, you reap what you sow.

These debts need to be dealt with. It is no good just saying to God that you repent. You have to pay back the debt in order to stop it from affecting your life negatively. Indeed, it is the right thing to do. When you don't know how to contact somebody in order to return their money, I suggest that you ask the Lord what to do and make a donation to a ministry or to whomever the Lord directs.

Sometimes people can get into debt through no fault of their own. This situation might be due to a financial recession in their country, which prevents them from earning a living.

Be assured that God is aware of these things, and He will help you restore your life if you are honest and you are endeavoring to do what He says.

Steps to get out of debt:

1. Pray and ask God to give you a plan to get out of debt.

2. Find a wise man or woman who can go through your financial affairs with you. This advisor should be a Christian who can help you turn your life around. Look for someone who is already successful, someone who will genuinely help you. Don't look for money from them! But look for wisdom and have a willingness to be accountable to them as you make progress. It is sometimes possible to find Christian debt counselors who may even be able to negotiate some of your debts away. However, it is best to pay everything back and to be honorable in every area of your finances.

3. Make a list of everybody you owe money to, and start paying them back.

4. Make ***absolutely sure*** that you give tithes of all your income. Don't make excuses and say, "Oh, this was a gift." Tithe ***everything*** that comes to you.

   9 "_____ the Lord with thy_____, and with the
   _____ of all thine increase:
   10 So shall thy barns be filled with plenty, and thy presses shall burst out with new wine.
   11 My son, despise not the chastening of the Lord; neither be weary of his correction:
   (Proverbs 3:9-11 KJV)

5. Make sure you are living righteously, and ask the Holy Spirit to convict you of any sin. As He does so, be sure to repent.

6. Increase your giving. Look for things in your house that you do not need, and give them away. Through giving you will unblock the blockages to your receiving.

7. Obedience. Ask God what He wants you to do. If you are finding it hard to hear, ask yourself this question: What was the last thing God asked me to do? Often we can become hard of hearing when

8. we simply don't do the last thing asked of us. Remember what it is was and do it!

9. Work hard. Make sacrifices and give.

Be successful and seek first the Kingdom of God.
(See Matthew 6:33.)

Reflections

1. Are we allowed to borrow?
2. How do we receive financial curses?
3. How do we get out of debt?

Memory Verses

"Owe no man any thing, but to love one another: for he that loveth another hath fulfilled the law."
(Romans 13:8 KJV)

9 "Honour the Lord with thy substance, and with the firstfruits of all thine increase:
10 So shall thy barns be filled with plenty, and thy presses shall burst out with new wine.
11 My son, despise not the chastening of the Lord; neither be weary of his correction:"
(Proverbs 3:9-11 KJV)

Closing Prayer

(If you are in debt.) Dear Father, have mercy and grace on me and please help release me from debt. Please give me a plan to get out of debt and provide me with counselors who can help lift me up. Show me any areas that I can work on so that I can be a contributor into your Kingdom. I thank you that you became poor so that I could become rich. Let my life bring praise and honor to You. I ask for these things in the name of Jesus. Amen.

(If you want to help those in debt.) Dear Father, thank you for your graciousness and love for the poor. Please give me a heart of tenderness to those in need, and a willingness to help those less blessed than myself. Show me those that I can help, and give me wisdom to lead them to your throne. I ask this in the name of Jesus. Amen.

My Garden
Chapter Seventeen – Study Guide

Opening Prayer

     Dear Father, You gave Adam a garden to tend, please teach me how I can tend my garden. I ask this in the name of Jesus. Amen

---

The following questions will be answered during study of this chapter:
1. Do farmers expect to receive something back when they sow in their fields?
2. Does that make them greedy?
3. Can I sow bad crops?

Growing My Garden

Those of you who know me will be very surprised that I am writing about my garden. *(I don't like gardening.)*

I do like using a garden and looking at a garden, but I always feel that I have something more important to do than gardening.

Perhaps this is symptomatic of the way we run our lives. I say this because when I talk about my garden, I am using it as a picture of my life.

God put Adam in the Garden of Eden, and his job was to tend it.

Primarily that is the job we all have—to tend our gardens.

We plant blessings in our life, and we plant curses in our lives.

What is growing in your life? Are they blessings, or are they curses that are sucking the life out of you? Very often, it may be both.

The blessings are like fruit trees, and the curses are like weeds, nettles, and thorns.

When you give, it is given back to you.

> *"Give, _____ _____ will be given to you: good measure, pressed down, shaken together, and running over will be put into your bosom. For with the same measure that you use, it will be measured back to you."*
> ***(Luke 6:38 NKJV)***

In my garden, I have a number of interesting trees. I have a motorbike tree, a watch tree, a helps tree, a television tree, a car tree, a thousand-pound note tree, a gold tree etc.

When you give, it is like a farmer sowing seed into his field. The seed grows and multiplies.

As I have sown the items I mention above by giving them away, they come back to me in seasons.

Reward of Obedience

One night the Lord woke me up and said that He had something important for me to do. I asked what it was, and He said that He wanted me to give a thousand pounds to another Christian brother. Well, at that time my business was under a lot of pressure, I had around four thousand pounds in the bank, but I had to pay out that week about six thousand pounds.

I had the money, but! The next morning I told my wife, who supported me, by saying, "If the Lord has said it, we had better do it." She's a good wife. We gave the money and the business survived. Now, every so often, somebody sends me a thousand pounds. This had never happened to me before. Nobody had ever given me money in those quantities before, but now suddenly I was receiving thousands of pounds from different sources. In total I have been given £48,000 since that day. Every now and again somebody would send me a thousand pounds.

I gave a £600 Gucci watch to someone who was down and out, and I received back a watch that was worth £1600.

I like this garden.

Please don't see this as just a means of getting things; however, it shows how the mechanics of sowing and reaping works. If you ask a farmer if he expects to receive something back by sowing into the ground, he would think you were mad. If you then said that he must be greedy by understanding how it works and applying it, he would doubly think you are mad.

You can be greedy with or without material wealth. A Christian's heart is judged by how he gives, not by how he receives.

As Paul said:

> 6 "But this I say: He who _____ _____ will also reap sparingly, and he who _____ _____ will also reap bountifully.

7 So let each one give as he purposes in his heart, not grudgingly or of necessity; for God loves a cheerful giver.
8 And God is able to make all grace abound toward you, that you, always having all sufficiency in all things, may have an abundance for every good work"
(2 Corinthians 9:6-8 NKJV)

Having seen that it worked, I decided that I would deliberately plant seeds in my garden.

First, I decided to plant a row of £100 bushes. I thought that the ground it was sown into would also be important. Better to sow into people and ministries who are in need, rather than simply giving to the rich. Also, I wanted to see how long it took for some seeds to prosper into fruit.

I gave a £100 to Rev. Hugh Osgood at Cornerstone Ministries. I asked that it be put towards going out for a meal, or anything else. The next day a member of Hugh Osgood's church, knowing nothing of "my gift," sent me £100 to use for my ministry. I had never received anything from anyone at Hugh's church before.

Was this a coincidence?

Now let's look at the more serious aspect of tending your garden.

Have you weeds, nettles, or thorns in your garden?

When you give, you receive back the good things. However, you also receive back the negative things.

Do you owe money to somebody? That can be like a tree bearing negative money in your life. Do you always have less money than you need? Do you wonder why you work hard, yet it's like having holes in your pockets.

The reason is that you have a big weed in your garden, and it is sucking money out of your life. Get rid of it!

Do some weeding. Weed out the debts, and pay them back. Don't solely ask God to forgive you, because you are still reaping the consequences.

True repentance is more than just saying "I'm sorry" to God. You need to make restitution.

Not only can we have weeds sucking the life out of the ground, but we can also have thorns that cause us pain.

Let us see what Jesus said about the thorns in the Parable of the Sowing of the Word.

150

"Now these are the ones sown among thorns; they are the ones who hear the word, "and _____ _____ _____ _____, *the* _____ _____ _____ _____, *and the* _____ *for other things entering in* choke the word, and it becomes unfruitful."*
(Mark 4:18-19 NKJV)

1. What three things makes the Word unfruitful?

     1. _____
     2. _____
     3. _____

Your garden can become unfruitful as a result of having cares in your life. Worry and anxieties only cause harm.

Root out all worries, and cares.

6 "Be _____ _____ _____, *but in everything by prayer and supplication, with thanksgiving, let your requests be made known to God;*
7 and the peace of God, which surpasses all understanding, will guard your hearts and minds through Christ Jesus."
 (Philippians 4:6-7 NKJV)

33"But seek first the kingdom of God and His righteousness, and all these things shall be added to you.
34 Therefore _____ _____ _____ **about tomorrow,** *for tomorrow will worry about its own things. Sufficient for the day is its own trouble."*
 (Matthew 6:33-34 NKJV)

6 "Therefore humble yourselves under the mighty hand of God, that He may exalt you in due time,
7 _____ _____ _____ _____
upon Him, *for He cares for you."*
(1 Peter 5:6-7 NKJV)

When you do your gardening and weeding, pull up every worry and anxiety you can find.

Be systematic and if necessary, do it daily.

The Deceitfulness of Riches—Thorns

Let's make this point as clear as possible—riches are fine. In fact, Jesus died to receive riches.

"As for every man to whom _____ has given riches and wealth, and given him power to eat of it, to receive his heritage and rejoice in his labor—this is the gift of God."
(Ecclesiastes 5:19 NKJV)

"Worthy is the Lamb who was slain to receive power and _____ and wisdom, And strength and honor and glory and blessing!"
(Revelation 5:12 NKJV)

What is not fine, however, is the worship of riches; this is described by Jesus as serving mammon.

"_____ _____ _____ _____ _____

_____; for either he will hate the one and love the other, or else he will be loyal to the one and despise the other. You cannot serve God and mammon."*
(Matthew 6:24 NKJV)

Seeking riches first is not the way of the Kingdom. You need to seek first the Kingdom of God and his righteousness. *(See Matthew 6:33.)*

*5 "...men of corrupt minds and destitute of the truth, who suppose that godliness is a means of gain. From such withdraw yourself.
6 Now godliness with contentment is great gain."*
(1 Timothy 6:5-6 NKJV)

Godliness is a means of great gain, but is not to be used solely for gain. God is not mocked; you can only serve one master.

> **Desires for other things entering in choke the Word, and it becomes unfruitful. These are the thorns.**

Strong desires, when they become greater than is morally acceptable, are described as *lusts*.

When you focus too much on a desire, there does not leave much room for focusing on what Jesus wants you to do and be. Therefore, desires which can be quite innocent in normal strength become distorted into negative forces. All too often our lives are being spent on vanity, and the time and force that are spent in pursuing vanities should be used for building God's kingdom. It is too easy to get sidetracked into the following of an idol, such as the pursuit of riches.

James puts it this way:

"From whence come wars and fightings among you? come they not hence, _____ _____ _____ _____ that war in your members? Ye lust, and have not: ye kill, and desire to have, and cannot obtain: ye fight and war, yet ye have not, because ye ask not. Ye ask, and receive not, because ye ask amiss, that ye may _____ _____ _____ _____ _____ ,,

(James 4:1-3 KJV)

Even our prayer can be contaminated through lusts!

Are your desires the desires God wants you to have? Are your ambitions, Gods' ambitions? If you are not sure, take them to the cross. Leave them there until God tells you to take them up.

What is growing in your garden? Is it blessings or curses?

Reflections
1. Do farmers expect to receive something back when they sow in their fields?
2. Does that make them greedy?
3. Can I sow bad crops?

Applications
Do some gardening, plant some good seed and uproot the bad.

Memory Verses
"Give, and it will be given to you: good measure, pressed down, shaken together, and running over will be put into your bosom. For with the same measure that you use, it will be measured back to you."
(Luke 6:38 NKJV)

6 *"But this I say: He who sows sparingly will also reap sparingly, and he who sows bountifully will also reap bountifully.*
(2 Corinthians 9:6 NKJV)

Closing Prayer

Dear Father, please help me to be diligent in knowing the state of my garden. Help me to plant the crops that you want me to be blessed by. Show me those that you want me to bless. Show me the weeds and thorns that need dealing with. I ask for these things in the name of Jesus. Amen

Keys to Prosperity, Good Provision, and Success
Chapter Eighteen – Study Guide

Opening Prayer
> Dear Lord, please help me to understand the keys to prosperity that You have placed in Your Word. Help me to understand the keys to poverty, so that I can avoid them and help others. I ask this in the name of Jesus. Amen.

The following questions will be answered during study of this chapter:
1. What are the keys to prosperity?
2. What are the keys to poverty?

> **These keys are for those who want to keep an eye on their lives and want to grow in their ability to help build God's kingdom.**

Write in the Keys to Prosperity
Key One
> *4 "And I will make thy seed to multiply as the stars of heaven, and will give unto thy seed all these countries; and in thy seed shall all the nations of the earth be blessed;*
> *5 Because that Abraham obeyed my voice, and kept my charge, my commandments, my statutes, and my laws."*
> **(Genesis 26:4-5 KJV)**

_____

Key Two
> *"In the house of the righteous is much treasure: but in the revenues of the wicked is trouble."*
> **(Proverbs 15:6 KJV)**

_____

Key Three
> *"By humility and the fear of the Lord are riches, and honour, and life."*
> **(Proverbs 22:4 KJV)**

_____

Key Four

> *"But seek ye first the kingdom of God, and his righteousness; and these things shall be added unto you."*
> **(Matthew 6:33 KJV)**

Key Five

> *"Bring ye all the tithes into the storehouse, that there may be meat in mine house, and prove me now herewith, saith the Lord of hosts, if I will not open you the windows of heaven, and pour you out a blessing, that there shall not be room enough to receive it."*
> **(Malachi 3:10 KJV)**

Key Six

> *"He that hath pity upon the poor lendeth unto the Lord; and that which he hath given will he pay him again."*
> **(Proverbs 19:17 KJV)**

Key Seven

> *"Only be thou strong and very courageous, that thou mayest observe to do according to all the law, which Moses my servant commanded thee: turn not from it to the right hand or to the left, that thou mayest prosper whithersoever thou goest."*
> **(Joshua 1:7 KJV)**

Key Eight

> *"Riches profit not in the day of wrath: but righteousness delivereth from death."*
> **(Proverbs 11:4 KJV)**

Key Nine

> *"The thoughts of the diligent tend only to plenteousness; but of every one that is hasty only to want."*
> **(Proverbs 21:5 KJV)**

Key Ten

"Death and life are in the power of the tongue: and they that love it shall eat the fruit thereof."
(Proverbs 18:21 KJV)

Key Eleven

Give, and it shall be given unto you; good measure, pressed down, and shaken together, and running over, shall men give into your bosom. For with the same measure that ye mete withal it shall be measured to you again." (Also remember the negative)
(Luke 6:38 KJV)

Key Twelve

'For the drunkard and the glutton shall come to poverty: and drowsiness shall clothe a man with rags."
(Proverbs 23:21 KJV)

Key Thirteen

"That ye be not slothful, but followers of them who through faith and patience inherit the promises."
(Hebrews 6:12 KJV)

Write in the Keys to Poverty
Key One

"Poverty and shame shall be to him that refuseth instruction: but he that regardeth reproof shall be honoured."
(Proverbs 13:18 KJV)

Key Two

"Honour thy father and thy mother, as the Lord thy God hath commanded thee; that thy days may be prolonged, and that it may go well with thee, in the land which the Lord thy God giveth thee."
(Deuteronomy 5:16 KJV)

Key Three

> *"The righteous eateth to the satisfying of his soul: but the belly of the wicked shall want."*
> **(Proverbs 13:25 KJV)**

Key Four

> *"By humility and the fear of the Lord are riches, and honour, and life."*
> **(Proverbs 22:4 KJV)**

Key Five

> *" He that loveth pleasure shall be a poor man: he that loveth wine and oil shall not be rich."*
> **(Proverbs 21:17 KJV)**

Key Six

> *"Will a man rob God? Yet ye have robbed me. But ye say, Wherein have we robbed thee? In tithes and offerings."*
> **(Malachi 3:8 KJV)**

Key Seven

> *"Whoso stoppeth his ears at the cry of the poor, he also shall cry himself, but shall not be heard."*
> **(Proverbs 21:13 KJV)**

Key Eight

> *"The lips of the righteous feed many: but fools die for want of wisdom."*
> **(Proverbs 10:21 KJV)**

Key Nine

> *9 "How long wilt thou sleep, O sluggard? when wilt thou arise out of thy sleep?*
> *10 Yet a little sleep, a little slumber, a little folding of the hands to sleep:*
> *11 So shall thy poverty come as one that travelleth, and thy want as an armed man."*
> **(Proverbs 6:9-11 KJV)**

Key Ten
"The thoughts of the diligent tend only to plenteousness; but of every one that is hasty only to want."
(Proverbs 21:5 KJV)

Key Eleven
"In the multitude of words there wanteth not sin: but he that refraineth his lips is wise."
(Proverbs 10:19 KJV)

Key Twelve
"Give, and it shall be given unto you; good measure, pressed down, and shaken together, and running over, shall men give into your bosom. For with the same measure that ye mete withal it shall be measured to you again."
(Luke 6:38 KJV)

Key Thirteen
"For the drunkard and the glutton shall come to poverty: and drowsiness shall clothe a man with rags."
(Proverbs 23:21 KJV)

Key Fourteen
"He that hasteth to be rich hath an evil eye, and considereth not that poverty shall come upon him."
(Proverbs 28:22 KJV)

Reflections
1. What are the keys to prosperity?
2. What are the keys to poverty?

Closing Prayer

Dear Father in Heaven, I truly want to be a child that brings you pleasure. Thank you that I am righteous through Jesus, but help me to be holy as You are holy. Help me to be submissive to Your Holy Spirit, that I may be obedient in all You have called me to, fearing You and seeking first Your Kingdom. I desire to be a good citizen of your Kingdom and I commit myself to bringing Your tithe to You, that Your Church will have food in it. Help me to give my offerings cheerfully without fear, knowing that Your love for me is forever.

I do not seek my own pleasures and will, but desire to do Yours. Open my eyes to the poor and unfortunate, those who need Your care. If I have borrowed from others, without returning, please show me, and I will make restitution.

Thank you for the treasures of Your Word. I will honor my parents and honor Your Word. Fill me with Your wisdom and knowledge, working diligently in Your scriptures and my daily tasks. Let me be a doer of Your Word and not simply a hearer. My tongue is Yours, help me to bridle it to Your glory. Let my words be full of life, sprinkling those around me with Your living waters.

Help me to be patient, to make wise plans, not rushing and hastening after riches. I reject mammon and choose to live for Thy Kingdom. I ask for the faith to receive the promises given to Abraham, Isaac, and Jacob. I pray for the peace of Jerusalem, and eagerly await the New Jerusalem. I love You Father, please help me to be a child that brings you pleasure. In Jesus' name. Amen.

Summary
Chapter Nineteen – Study Guide

Having read this far through this study guide you must be serious about prospering. The Scriptures are clear; God wants His children to prosper, even as their soul prospers. I sincerely hope that you take the admonition to heart to be doers of the word, and not just hearers, desiring the pure milk of the word, and growing.

At this point in time, I am forty-eight years old, the Lord has given me just about everything I have ever wanted, and I have tried my best to give Him everything He has wanted from me.

There is nothing like working for God, no fulfilment to be compared with working for the King of Kings.

He is able to make all grace abound toward you; that you always having all sufficiency in all things, may abound to every good work.

So press on toward the mark for your prize in the high calling of God in Christ Jesus.

> *"Beloved, I wish above all things that thou mayest prosper and be in health, even as thy soul prospereth."*
> *(3 John 1:2 KJV)*

> 22 *"But be ye doers of the word, and not hearers only, deceiving your own selves.*
> 23 *For if any be a hearer of the word, and not a doer, he is like unto a man beholding his natural face in a glass."*
> *(James 1:22-23 KJV)*

> *"As newborn babes, desire the sincere milk of the word, that ye may grow thereby."*
> *(1 Peter 2:2 KJV)*

> *"And God is able to make all grace abound toward you; that ye, always having all sufficiency in all things, may abound to every good work."*
> *(2 Corinthians 9:8 KJV)*

> *"I press toward the mark for the prize of the high calling of God in Christ Jesus."*
> *(Philippians 3:14 KJV)*

Glossary
Chapter Twenty – Study Guide

Definitions of Hebrew, Aramaic and Greek words for prosperity from Strong's Exhaustive Concordance of the Bible

Strong's Reference No. 06743

צָלַח - tsalach

1) to rush
2) to advance, prosper, make progress, succeed, be profitable
2a) to prosper
2b) to make prosperous, bring to successful issue, cause to prosper
2b2) to show or experience prosperity, prosper

Sample scriptures using *tsalach*:

"The keeper of the prison looked not to anything that was under his hand; because the LORD was with him, and that which he did, the LORD made it to prosper."
(Genesis 39:23 KJV)

"This book of the law shall not depart out of thy mouth; but thou shalt meditate therein day and night, that thou mayest observe to do according to all that is written therein: for then thou shalt make thy way prosperous, and then thou shalt have good success."
(Joshua 1:8 KJV)

Strong's Reference No. 02896

טוֹב - towb

1) good, pleasant, agreeable
1a) pleasant, agreeable (to the senses)
1b) pleasant (to the higher nature)
1c) good, excellent (of its kind)
1d) good, rich, valuable in estimation
1e) good, appropriate, becoming

1f) better (comparative)
1g) glad, happy, prosperous (of man's sensuous nature)
1h) good understanding (of man's intellectual nature)
1i) good, kind, benign
1j) good, right (ethical) n m
2) a good thing, benefit, welfare
2a) welfare, prosperity, happiness
2b) good things (collective)
2c) good, benefit
2d) moral good n f
3) welfare, benefit, good things
3a) welfare, prosperity, happiness
3b) good things (collective)
3c) bounty

Sample Scriptures using *towb*:

I have included this verse for "towb," which is translated as "good," as it gives a good understanding as to how God uses the word.

> *"And God saw the light, that it was good: and God divided the light from the darkness."*
> *(Genesis 1:4 KJV)*

> *"Howbeit I believed not the words, until I came, and mine eyes had seen it: and, behold, the half was not told me: thy wisdom and prosperity exceedeth the fame which I heard."*
> *(1 Kings 10:7 KJV)*

> *"Cry yet, saying, Thus saith the LORD of hosts; My cities through prosperity shall yet be spread abroad; and the LORD shall yet comfort Zion, and shall yet choose Jerusalem."*
> *(Zechariah 1:17 KJV)*

Strong's Reference No. 07965

שָׁלוֹם - shalowm

1) completeness, soundness, welfare, peace
1a) completeness (in number)
1b) safety, soundness (in body)
1c) welfare, health, prosperity
1d) peace, quiet, tranquility, contentment
1e) peace, friendship
1e1) of human relationships

1e2) with God especially in covenant relationship
1f) peace (from war)
1g) peace (as adjective)

Sample Scriptures using *shalowm*:

>*"And thus you shall say to him who lives in prosperity: 'Peace be to you, peace to your house, and peace to all that you have!"*
>**(1 Samuel 25:6 NKJV)**

Strong's Reference No. 06744

צְלַח - tslach (Aramaic)

1) to prosper
1a) (Aphel) 1a1) to cause to prosper
1a2) show prosperity, be prosperous, have success, be successful

Sample Scripture using *tslach*:

>*"Be it known unto the king, that we went into the province of Judea, to the house of the great God, which is builded with great stones, and timber is laid in the walls, and this work goeth fast on, and prospereth in their hands."*
>**(Ezra 5:8 KJV)**

Strong's Reference No. 07999

שָׁלַם – shalam

1) to be in a covenant of peace, be at peace
1a) (Qal) 1a1) to be at peace
1a2) peaceful one (participle)
1b) (Pual) one in covenant of peace (participle)
1c) (Hiphil) 1c1) to make peace with
1c2) to cause to be at peace
1d) (Hophal) to live in peace
2) to be complete, be sound
2a) (Qal) 2a1) to be complete, be finished, be ended
2a2) to be sound, be uninjured
2b) (Piel) 2b1) to complete, finish

2b2) to make safe
2b3) to make whole or good, restore, make compensation
2b4) to make good, pay
2b5) to requite, recompense, reward
2c) (Pual) 2c1) to be performed
2c2) to be repaid, be requited
2d) (Hiphil)
2d1) to complete, perform
2d2) to make an end of

Sample Scripture using *shalam*:

> *"If thou wert pure and upright; surely now he would awake for thee, and make the habitation of thy righteousness prosperous. Though thy beginning was small, yet thy latter end should greatly increase."*
> ***(Job 8:6-7 KJV)***

Strong's Reference No. 07951

שָׁלָה - shalah

1) to be at rest, prosper, be quiet, be at ease
1a) (Qal) 1a1) to be or have quiet
1a2) to be at ease, prosper

Sample scripture using *shalah*:

> *"Pray for the peace of Jerusalem: they shall prosper that love thee. Peace be within thy walls, and prosperity within thy palaces."*
> ***(Psalm. 122:6-7 KJV)***

Strong's Reference No. 07959

שֶׁלֶו - shelev

1) ease, prosperity

Sample scripture using *shelev*:

> *"And in my prosperity I said, I shall never be moved."*
> ***(Psalm 30:6 KJV)***

Strong's Reference No. 07961

שָׁלֵו – shalev

1) quiet, at ease, prosperous
1a) at ease (of persons)
1b) quiet (of land)
1c) quiet, ease
1d) ease (subst)

Sample scripture using *shalev*:

> *"Behold, these are the ungodly, who prosper in the world; they increase in riches."*
> **(Psalm. 73:12 KJV)**

Strong's Reference No. 07962

שַׁלְוָה - shalvah

1) quietness, ease, prosperity

Sample Scriptures using *shalvah*:

> *"Pray for the peace of Jerusalem: they shall prosper that love thee. Peace be within thy walls, and prosperity within thy palaces."*
> **(Psalm. 122:6-7 KJV)**

> *"In the day of prosperity be joyful, but in the day of adversity consider: God also hath set the one over against the other, to the end that man should find nothing after him"*
> **(Ecclesiastes 7:14 KJV)**

Strong's Reference No. 03787

כָּשֵׁר – kasher

1) to succeed, please, be suitable, be proper, be advantageous, be right and proper to
1a) (Qal) to please, be proper
1b) (Hiphil) to give success

Sample scripture using *kasher*:

> *"In the morning sow thy seed, and in the evening withhold not thine hand: for thou knowest not whether shall prosper, either this or that, or whether they both shall be alike good."*
> *(Ecclesiastes 11:6 KJV)*

Strong's Reference No. 2137

εὐοδόω euodoo

1) to grant a prosperous and expeditious journey, to lead by a direct and easy way
2) to grant a successful issue, to cause to prosper
3) to prosper, be successful

All scriptures using *euodoo*:

> *"Making request, if by any means now at length I might have a prosperous journey by the will of God to come unto you."*
> *(Romans 1:10 KJV)*

> *"Upon the first day of the week let every one of you lay by him in store, as God hath prospered (2137) him, that there be no gatherings when I come."*
> *(1 Corinthians 16:2 KJV)*

> *"Beloved, I wish above all things that thou mayest prosper and be in health, even as thy soul prospereth."*
> *(3 John 1:2 KJV)*

Financial Balance Sheet

In all changes to our life, whether it be dieting, exercise, or intercession, we need to measure our results. Even small improvements give us the opportunity to thank God and be encouraged as we move towards our goals. Please note that it may take a number of years for the effects that positive changes in our lifestyles produce. But God is always faithful to our desire to live a Godly life in our finances.

With that in mind we need to know what our starting position is, which is why we need to produce a financial balance sheet. A balance sheet is simply a snapshot of our present financial position taking into account our assets and liabilities. This may be a positive or negative figure.

First of all we need to add up all our assets.

PLEASE FILL IN YOUR OWN FIGURES IN THE (   )

	Example		Your Own
Cash and Bank Accounts			
Checking account	796	-	( )
Checking account	50	-	( )
Savings account	3,500	-	( )
Savings account	2,000	-	( )
Other		-	( )
Real Estate			
176 High Street	125,000	-	( )
Rose Cottage	80,000	-	( )
Other		-	( )
Vehicles			
Car 1	18,000	-	( )
Car 2	5,000	-	( )
Motorbike	4,000	-	( )
Other			
Stocks-Shares-Pensions			
Roth IRA/Pension	6,000	-	( )
Stocks/Shares	2,000	-	( )
Life Insurance		-	( )
Other		-	( )
Miscellaneous (High value items, house contents, art, antiques etc..)			
Musical Instruments	1,500	-	( )
Jewelry	2,000	-	( )
Other		-	( )
Total Assets	**249,846**	**Total Assets**	( )

Next we need to add up our liabilities.

PLEASE FILL IN YOUR OWN FIGURES IN THE (   )

	Example		Your Own	
Real Estate (Mortgage)				
176 High Street	85,000	-	(	)
Rose Cottage	50,000	-	(	)
Other		-	(	)
Loans and Credit Cards				
Automobile Loan 1	12,000	-	(	)
Automobile Loan 2	3,000	-	(	)
Motorbike Loan	2,000	-	(	)
Personal Loan		-	(	)
Student Loan		-	(	)
Credit Card 1		-	(	)
Credit Card 2		-	(	)
Other		-	(	)
Other		-	(	)

Total Liabilities   152,00   **Total Liabilities**   (   )

By subtracting our total liabilities, from our total assets, we have a figure that indicates our earthly financial wealth. As previously stated this may be positive or negative.

In the example above that would be 249,846 – 152,000 = 97,846

Please fill in your own figures below:

My total assets (**) Minus My Total Liabilities (**   **) = (**   **) My Total wealth.**

This exercise is worth doing once a month, as many of the figures will remain the same, it should only take about 5 minutes. But that 5 minutes will provide the encouragement that will set you towards your goals.

Scriptural Quotations Index
Arranged by Book with Chapter Number

Memory Verses by Chapter

Chapter 01

"Let them shout for joy, and be glad, that favour my righteous cause: yea, let them say continually, Let the Lord be magnified, which hath pleasure in the prosperity of his servant."
(Psalm 35:27 KJV)

"Beloved, I wish above all things that thou mayest prosper and be in health, even as thy soul prospereth."
(3 John 1:2 KJV)

Chapter 02

"That ye be not slothful, but followers of them who through faith and patience inherit the promises."
(Hebrews 6:12 KJV)

"And if ye be Christ's, then are ye Abraham's seed, and heirs according to the promise."
(Galatians 3:29 KJV)

Chapter 03

"...and as long as he sought the Lord, God made him to prosper."
(2 Chronicles 26:5b KJV)

"So David inquired of the Lord, saying, "Shall I go up against the Philistines? Will You deliver them into my hand?..."
(2 Samuel 5:19a NKJV)

Chapter 04

"For the love of money is the root of all evil: which while some coveted after, they have erred from the faith, and pierced themselves through with many sorrows."
(I Timothy 6:10 KJV)

Chapter 05

"Give, and it shall be given unto you; good measure, pressed down, and shaken together, and running over, shall men give into your bosom. For with the same measure that ye mete withal it shall be measured to you again".
(Luke 6:38 KJV)

Chapter 06

7 *"Only be thou strong and very courageous, that thou mayest observe to   do according to all the law, which Moses my servant commanded thee: whithersoever thou goest.*
8 *This book of the law shall not depart out of thy mouth; but thou shalt   meditate   therein   day and night, that thou mayest observe to do according to all that is written therein: for then thou shalt   make   thy   way   prosperous,   and   then   thou   shalt   have   good   success."*
(Joshua 1:7-8 KJV)

Chapter 07

"And all the tithe of the land, whether of the seed of the land, or of the fruit of the tree, is the Lord's: it is holy unto the Lord."
(Leviticus 27:30 KJV)

"Will a man rob God? Yet ye have robbed me. But ye say, Wherein have we robbed thee? In tithes and offerings."
(Malachi 3:8 KJV)

10 *Bring ye all the tithes into the storehouse, that there may be meat in mine house, and prove me now herewith, saith the Lord of hosts, if I will not open you the windows of heaven, and pour you out a blessing, that there shall not be room enough to receive it.*
11 *And I will rebuke the devourer for your sakes, and he shall not destroy the fruits of your ground; neither shall your vine cast her fruit before the time in the field, saith the Lord of hosts.*
(Malachi 3:10-11 KJV)

Chapter 08

"Verily, verily, I say unto you, Except a corn of wheat fall into the ground and die, it abideth alone: but if it die, it bringeth forth much fruit."
(John 12:24 KJV)

"For he that soweth to his flesh shall of the flesh reap corruption; but he that soweth to the Spirit shall of the Spirit reap life everlasting."
(Galatians 6:8 KJV)

"But this I say, He which soweth sparingly shall reap also sparingly; and he which soweth bountifully shall reap also bountifully."
(2 Corinthians 9:6 KJV)

Chapter 09

"How long will you _____ to go and_____ the land which the LORD God of your fathers has_____ you?"
(Joshua. 18:3b NKJV)

"_____the good fight of faith, _____ _____ on eternal life, to which you were also called and have confessed the good confession in the presence of many witnesses."
(1 Timothy 6:12 NKJV)

And from the days of John the Baptist until now the kingdom of heaven suffereth violence, and the violent take it by force.
(Matthew 11:12 KJV)

Chapter 10

"In Christ Jesus the blessing of Abraham might come to the Gentiles, so that we would receive the promise of the Spirit through faith."
(Galatians 3:14 NASB)

"He who did not spare His own Son, but delivered Him up for us all, how will He not also with Him freely give us all things?"
(Romans 8:32 NKJV)

*"Blessed be the God and Father of our Lord Jesus Christ, **who has blessed us with all spiritual blessings in the heavenly places in Christ...** 5 having predestined us to adoption as sons by Jesus Christ to Himself."*
(Ephesians 1:3 & 5 NKJV)

*16b **"By myself I have sworn,** says the LORD, because you have done this thing, and have not withheld your son, your only son—*
17 "blessing I will bless you, and multiplying I will multiply your descendants as the stars of the heaven and as the sand which is on the seashore; and your descendants shall possess the gate of their enemies. 18 "In your seed all the nations of the earth shall be blessed, because you have obeyed My voice."
(Genesis 22:16-18 NKJV)

Chapter 11

"Giving thanks unto the Father, which hath made us meet to be partakers of the inheritance of the saints in light:"
(Colossians 1:12 KJV)

"Blessed are the meek: for they shall inherit the earth."
(Matthew 5:5 KJV)

"Knowing that of the Lord ye shall receive the reward of the inheritance: for ye serve the Lord Christ."
(Colossians 3:24 KJV)

Chapter 12

"Now faith is the substance of things hoped for, the evidence of things not seen."
(Hebrews 11:1 KJV)

"But without faith it is impossible to please him: for he that cometh to God must believe that he is, and that he is a rewarder of them that diligently seek him."
(Hebrews 11:6 KJV)

"So then faith cometh by hearing, and hearing by the word of God."
(Romans 10:17 KJV)

"For by grace are ye saved through faith; and that not of yourselves: it is the gift of God:"

(Ephesians 2:8 KJV)

Chapter 13

"But you, O man of God, flee these things and pursue righteousness, godliness, faith, love, patience, gentleness."
(1 Timothy 6:11 NKJV)

"The end of a matter is better than its beginning, and patience is better than pride."
(Ecclesiastes 7:8 NIV)

2 "My brethren, count it all joy when you fall into various trials,
3 knowing that the testing of your faith produces patience,
4 But let patience have its perfect work, that you may be perfect and complete, lacking nothing"
(James 1:2-4 NKJV)

Chapter 14

*33 "**But seek ye first the kingdom of God, and his righteousness**; and all these things shall be added unto you."*
 (Matthew 6:33 KJV)

*34 "Take therefore no thought for the morrow: for the morrow shall take thought for the things of itself. Sufficient unto the day is the evil thereof." **(Matthew 6:34 KJV)***

7 "Casting all your care upon him; for he careth for you."
(I Peter 5:7 KJV)

6 "Be careful for nothing; but in every thing by prayer and supplication with thanksgiving let your requests be made known unto God.
7 And the peace of God, which passeth all understanding, shall keep your hearts and minds through Christ Jesus."
 (Philippians 4:6-7 KJV)

Chapter 15

"For ye know the grace of our Lord Jesus Christ, that, though he was rich, yet for your sakes he became poor, that ye through his poverty might be rich."
(2 Corinthians 8:9 KJV)

*"**He that hath pity upon the poor lendeth unto the LORD;** and that which he hath given will he pay him again*
(Proverbs 19:17 KJV)

"The Lord maketh poor, and maketh rich: he bringeth low, and lifteth up."
(1 Samuel 2:7 KJV)

Chapter 16

"Owe no man any thing, but to love one another: for he that loveth another hath fulfilled the law."
(Romans 13:8 KJV)

9 "Honour the Lord with thy substance, and with the firstfruits of all thine increase:
10 So shall thy barns be filled with plenty, and thy presses shall burst out with new wine.
11 My son, despise not the chastening of the Lord; neither be weary of his correction:"
(Proverbs 3:9-11 KJV)

Chapter 17

"Give, and it will be given to you: good measure, pressed down, shaken together, and running over will be put into your bosom. For with the same measure that you use, it will be measured back to you."
(Luke 6:38 NKJV)

6 "But this I say: He who sows sparingly will also reap sparingly, and he who sows bountifully will also reap bountifully.
(2 Corinthians 9:6 NKJV)

Chapter 18

(None - Keys to Prosperity and Proverty)

Chapter 19

"Beloved, I wish above all things that thou mayest prosper and be in health, even as thy soul prospereth."
(3 John 1:2 KJV)

22 "But be ye doers of the word, and not hearers only, deceiving your own selves.
23 For if any be a hearer of the word, and not a doer, he is like unto a man beholding his natural face in a glass."
(James 1:22-23 KJV)

"As newborn babes, desire the sincere milk of the word, that ye may grow thereby."
(1 Peter 2:2 KJV)

"And God is able to make all grace abound toward you; that ye, always having all sufficiency in all things, may abound to every good work."
(2 Corinthians 9:8 KJV)

"I press toward the mark for the prize of the high calling of God in Christ Jesus."
(Philippians 3:14 KJV)

Chapter 20
(None – Glossary)

About the Author

Martin Powell is presently a musician, minister, preacher, teacher, author and businessman. He was born in London, England. His grew up in Nottingham where he studied music—specializing in the clarinet, winning many prizes. Obtaining a music scholarship, he travelled to London to study with Georgina Dobree at the *Royal Academy of Music*, from 1981-1985, and with Guy Deplus, Professor at the *Paris Conservatoire*, from 1985-1986.

In 1983, he went on to be the first clarinettist to win both the Hawke's clarinet prize and the John Solomon Wind Soloist prize in the same year. Also being awarded the Leslie Martin Scholarship for Clarinet; winner of the Nicholas Blake ensemble Prize; winner of a major award from the Ian Fleming Trust; and finalist in the Haverhill Sinfonia Soloist competition.

He first came to international recognition as a prize winner in the International Clarinet Congress Competition in London in 1984 and winning "Best Musician" in the International Christian Arts for God Competition 2007. He has gone on to perform in England, Germany, Austria, France, Italy, Spain and the USA.

He was also the principal clarinet player with the Henry Wood Chamber Orchestra. His clarinet playing has brought him to the attention of many composers. He has given World Premieres of many pieces; both Peter Heron and Wilfred Josephs have written pieces for him. Wilfred Joseph's First and Second sonatas were written for Martin and dedicated to him. The two sonatas were given world premieres at St. John's Smith Square, and the Harrogate International Music festival. Peter's "SoundBits" being premiered at the Purcell Room on the South Bank in September 1996. Other first performances of works by Joseph Horovitz, Mark Andrews, Barton Armstrong, David Llewelyn Green, Christopher Steel and Marjoijn Anstey. Martin has performed many concertos internationally and at home in the United Kingdom.

He has also recorded the music of Debussy, Poulenc, Stravinsky, and many other composers. As a committed Christian, Martin has dedicated all of his music to God including the many songs the Lord has given to him.

Martin Powell came back to the Lord at the age of twenty during the blossoming height of his music career. Being passionate to know God, and being obedient to the calling of the Lord, he sacrificially laid down his clarinet playing in order to know the Lord and to spend time deeply studying the Scriptures, which he has studied intensively for many years.

The Lord then took Martin into business, inspiring him to believe for a three-story music store, which the Lord gave him when he was penniless. Now Martin is promoting other Christians in business with the website **ChurchTalents.com**, coming soon. He is also the owner of Kingdom Talents Gold and Silver investments, specializing in gold and silver bullion, and rare coins. **Kingdom-Talents.com**

From 1993 to 2010 Martin was the Pastor of the New Haven Fellowship in London. This led to many preaching engagements across the wide spectrum of denominations and independent churches. His preaching has also been transmitted on the Gospel Channel through the Sky Satellite Network.

Out of his study of the Scriptures, the Lord began to give him fresh revelation about the subject of money. In obedience to the Lord, Martin Powell has written this study guide about money matters in God's Kingdom that is now in your hands. Jesus asked him to write the book as 'a favour to Him'. It is full of the living Word of God which he prays will be a blessing to you as you apply the principles of this book to your life.

Supplemental Material Available Soon

If you are interested in purchasing Martin's published works or music, you can find them at www.Kingdom-Talents.com/MartinPowell

To correspond with Martin Powell, please send your letter via email to: Martin@Kingdom-Talents.com. You may also contact us in writing at: Martin Powell, c/o Kingdom Talents, 375 StarLight Drvie, Fort Mill, SC 29715 USA

We would love to hear from you, and welcome your comments. If you desire Martin to come and minister the Word of God and perform his music in your Church, please mention this when you write.

Made in the USA
Columbia, SC
09 November 2024

46086167R00104